Stuart Taylor's new book, *How to Ace A Job Interview!*, is the perfect resource for the interview process. This IS the ace in the hole that will insure you getting the job you really want. Clearly explained, written with humor, yet full of excellent advice and tips, this book is a sure fire way to take the sweaty palms out of the interview proceedings and let you control your own destiny. It is bound to go to the top of the charts for how-to business books.

—Joan Ripley,
Pres. Chappaqua Bookshop and a Former
President of the American Booksellers Association

HOW TO ACE A JOB INTERVIEW!

HOW TO ACE A JOB INTERVIEW!

QUICK TIPS FOR AN EXCELLENT INTERVIEW

STUART C. TAYLOR

TATE PUBLISHING
AND ENTERPRISES, LLC

Published by Tate Publishing & Enterprises, LLC
127 E. Trade Center Terrace | Mustang, Oklahoma 73064 USA
1.888.361.9473 | www.tatepublishing.com

Tate Publishing is committed to excellence in the publishing industry. The company reflects the philosophy established by the founders, based on Psalm 68:11,
"The Lord gave the word and great was the company of those who published it."

Book design copyright © 2013 by Tate Publishing, LLC. All rights reserved.
Cover design by Lauro Talibong
Interior design by Mary Jean Archival

Published in the United States of America

ISBN: 978-1-62510-937-8
1. Business & Economics / Careers / Job Hunting
13.03.27

ACKNOWLEDGMENTS

Thank God for the wisdom and insight to write this book. Thanks to everyone I've ever interviewed for giving me the experience; thanks to friends and family for their invaluable input, and special thanks to my mom for her countless hours of encouragement and support.

I wish nothing less than the best of success to you all.

Contents

Section IV – Post-Interview

Section V – Get Fired Up!

INTRODUCTION

I often wondered why it took me over ten years to release this book when, essentially, the majority of the text had been completed in 2001. But then something happened that made it all very clear, something that needed to happen. Although unexpected, it was necessary for this manuscript to be truly finished. After years of teaching people how to ace their own job interviews as a recruiter and interview coach, there came a time when I had to put my own advice to the test.

For over a decade, I had a successful recruitment and training business, Top Performers Recruitment & Training, Inc. An integral part of my services, which set me apart from many of my colleagues, was that after identifying the best possible candidate for a position, I would often spend several hours personally preparing each candidate for his or her upcoming interviews. With anywhere from five to twenty-five candidates going out on interviews in a week sometimes, it was a time-consuming but invaluable part of the process that I committed to for my candidates' success. I had earned an excellent reputation in the industry and was recognized as a preferred recruiter by many major firms.

By 2009, however, the economy had taken its toll on my recruitment and training business. My largest client, Pfizer

Pharmaceuticals, Inc., (where I had placed more than an entire region's worth of personnel), as well as several other key clients, were downsizing and no longer in need of my placement services.

This was a stunning blow and a nerve-racking experience, not just to be losing my livelihood, but to think that after twenty-five years in the workforce, (including eleven at my own recruitment firm), I now had to go through the interview process myself. I was terrified.

The stress welled up inside of me, as it often does with people going out on an interview for the first time, second time, or any time. So this was what people experienced? The fear of not having interviewed for so long and the doubts that rose up within me were an unnerving reality.

Then it dawned on me. I'd been teaching people how to ace their job interviews for eleven years with an impeccable track record of success. Even those that I had coached but did not place directly through my firm called me back to say thank you that I had given them "the best interview advice ever," and that although I didn't place them myself, they ultimately landed a job because of the invaluable information I had shared with them.

In eleven years, I never had a complaint, not one single complaint on my interview training. I received comments like "you're the best recruiter I've ever worked with," "the information you shared was exactly what happened on the interview," "I got the job" over and over again. Even people who thought they couldn't learn anything were tremendously appreciative. All said my interview preparation training was excellent. But would it work for me?

It was time for me to put my own advice to the ultimate test.

I approached the interview process by applying precisely the very same interview tips I had been giving all my clients. I maneuvered through the interview process confidently as I incorporated the exact principles outlined in this book each step of the way. I was elated to find that *all* the tips I'd been teaching others for years worked for me too!

Not once, but twice, I landed a management job the first time out of the gate, and within two years repeated the process, landing an even better-paying job, which doubled my income. Two for two!

I have recently revived my business, and for this book to truly be a totally finished, credible work, it was important for me to know firsthand exactly what interviewees are experiencing. So now, in addition to the hundreds of testimonials from people I have assisted over the years, the circle is complete and my own experience corroborates that these are proven tips that work! I can now say that I am entirely confident they will work for you as well.

Be careful. These tips will work! Just be sure it's the job you want, because if you apply these tips, *you're gonna get this job*!

God has given each of us our own
unique set of skills, strengths and experiences.
And for very good reason.
Someone out there needs them.
My goal is to help you recognize and present
those distinctive and exceptional qualities
so they shine like polished gold
and employers can't help but realize
that you are the answer to their question.
You are what they are looking for.
You are the one for the job.

SECTION I

UNDERSTANDING THE INTERVIEW PROCESS

Section I, Chapter 1

HOW THIS BOOK WILL HELP YOU

After interviewing thousands of people throughout my twenty-plus year career as a regional sales trainer, sales manager, and professional recruiter, I found that while most candidates seem to have the ability to do the jobs they are applying for, the majority never make it past the first interview. Why?

While ability is critical, it is also relative. Ability alone, without the skills needed to navigate your way through the interviewing process, would be like Michael Jordan's having been unable to find his way from the locker room bench and onto the court. Without knowing how to get there, all his God-given abilities and gifts would never have been recognized by anyone.

Most people are surprised when they aren't called back for a second interview. They don't even know what disqualified them, particularly when they didn't make any noticeable blunders. What could it be then? *How to Ace a Job Interview!* will help take the mystery out of interviewing, as well as the anxiety associated with being unprepared or uncertain. It will help you understand what is required to be successful, including learning what employers are looking for from you. It will teach you how to avoid the disqualifiers and slam-dunk your interviews. Whether you are new to the job market or you have been interviewing for a while, this book is for you. After all, even the best and most experienced players still need a good coach!

A UNIQUE PERSPECTIVE

How to Ace a Job Interview! is your interview coach, your source of encouragement, and your personal guide to an outstanding interview. It is designed in an easy-to-read primarily bullet-point format to serve as a quick reference to important points. It is separated into convenient sections for easy reference so, depending on where you are in the interview process, you can quickly access the information you need when you need it. Often, with hectic schedules, obligations, or just short notice, there is not a lot of time to prepare for an interview. This book was written with that in mind. Additional information is available to provide a more thorough explanation of key points as time permits.

BE ENCOURAGED

To get you started on the right track, keep this in mind: if you have gotten a call for an interview, the company has pre-approved your résumé, which means, on paper, you've already met the minimum requirements. So relax. If you have a lot of time to prepare, read the whole book. If you don't, read the bullet points. Read it, reread it, study it, glance at it. However you use it, you'll get no-nonsense, straight-to-the-point, and proven tips that work. By the time you've reviewed the information in this book, you will know precisely *how to ace a job interview!*

In fact, after finishing this book, you may actually feel excited about your next interview. So let go of that stress and get ready for the best interview of your life!

THE "LITTLE THINGS"

DON'T LET THE "LITTLE THINGS" GET YOU!

Often, two or more equally qualified people are interviewed for the same position. One person gets it; the other does not. Why? It's simple: the "little things." It's often the "little things" that make the difference between a good interview and a great interview, a first interview and a final interview. Had you just done "this" or hadn't done "that," it would have made all the difference between a job offer and starting over.

Many of these deal breakers are avoidable. They range from things as obvious as not knowing enough about a company or fumbling on a response, to more subtle nuances, such as imperfect grammar, glancing away at the wrong time, a poor handshake, or forgetting to ask for a business card. Make no mistake, everything counts, even the seemingly little things.

Any action or inaction that prevents you from taking the next step, no matter how seemingly small, is a major mistake.

The following analogy will help illustrate the significance of this concept.

If you were considering buying a large, expensive, meticulously crafted piece of art, but discovered it had a tiny speck of an imperfection in it, what do you think you would you focus on? The speck, of course. Your opinion of the piece would immediately change. You would no longer see it as an otherwise flawless and expertly crafted, intricately detailed masterpiece but rather a flawed work with an unsightly splotch. Because of this little tiny speck, this imperfect work would instantly lose some or all of its value to you. Similarly, when an employer sees even a "speck" of an imperfection in you as a candidate, the employer will focus on that imperfection, and you lose value to that employer. It is human nature to focus on the imperfections, no matter how small. By contrast, if there were a duplicate piece of artwork available with no speck, which one would you want? Undoubtedly, it would be the speck-free piece. Interviewers operate under the same principle when comparing you to other candidates, which is why it is essential to present yourself as a perfect fit and have an interview as flawless as possible.

So do they want you to be *perfect*?

A perfect human being, *no*, a perfect fit for the job, *yes*. And that is precisely what this book is designed to do: help you to present yourself not as a "Good" fit, not as a "Very Good" fit, but as the "*Perfect Fit*" for the position and company you are being interviewed for.

Just as seemingly small details can make a negative impression, they are also essential ingredients in making a very positive impression. We've all experienced the difference a smile, a note, even a word can make in our personal lives. The same holds true on an interview. Similar to a relationship, it is often the smallest things that make the biggest difference. Keep this personalized perspective in mind to help you better understand the dynamics between you and your interviewer. An interviewer is a person with needs, wants, expectations, feelings, desires—*just like you*. By understanding these fundamental needs for yourself, you will better understand the needs of the interviewer. It's that simple. The next chapter, "The Dating Analogy," will further illustrate this point and help pave the way for one of the best interviews of your life.

Section I, Chapter 3

THE DATING ANALOGY

Dating is a concept we can all relate to. This analogy is designed to help you "get it" on a personal level. Reflecting on the principles and commonalities of this analogy will help you navigate through the interview process like nothing else!

The key principle is this:

> The dynamic between interviewer and interviewee is virtually identical to that of two people in an accelerated dating relationship exploring the possibility of marriage…(minus the romance).

The parallels are uncanny, which is why the *dating analogy* is so helpful. It allows you to take the mystery out of interviewing by looking at it as something basic that we all do or have done, some better than others perhaps, but regardless, we all understand the fundamentals from our own experiences. All you have to do is simply apply this analogy to the interviewing process.

Notice the commonalities. You search. You find each other. You meet. You explore. You ask questions. You test.

You observe. You challenge. You verify. You develop trust—or doubts. You laugh. You share, all in an effort to move to the next level—or not. You hope. You explore the past. You look at the "little things." You formulate opinions based on appearance, personality, ability to communicate, desire, past experiences, commonalities, feedback from others. You want to be desired and found interesting. You seek reassurance that they are who they say they are and that they mean what they say they mean. You look for tangible examples of truth in everything they say and do.

Why do you do all this? You're looking for someone with whom you feel comfortable, whom you can trust, and with whom you can grow harmoniously into the future. You want someone who meets your needs and adds value to your life. You want to see if the other person is a *perfect match* for you. These fundamental needs are the same in both interviewing and dating. Not only are the needs the same, but also the feelings of trust, confidence, commitment, and hope are the same.

THE VALUE OF THE DATING ANALOGY

To be successful on your interviews, it is imperative you understand the interviewer's perspective, needs, and triggers. By keeping the *dating analogy* parallels in mind, there will be practically no interview circumstance, situation, or question you can't manage appropriately—perfectly, in fact. You will know *exactly* how to conduct yourself throughout the interviewing process, even when you don't have this book to refer to! For some of you, this book will kill two birds with one stone: enhance your interviewing skills, landing you a job, and improve your dating skills, possibly landing you a spouse!

The following scenario illustrates the parallels between interviewing and dating and will help you understand how you are perceived on an interview.

Imagine you are on a date, considering marriage, and you ask your date with enthusiastic anticipation, "So why do you want to marry me?" And your date says, "Because you're the right height." How would you feel? Not too special. Certainly not like moving forward with that person. Even if the person added "and you're a brunette; I love brunettes." Your date's response is so grossly vague that besides being offensive, it's laughable. Essentially, your date communicated to you that there is nothing uniquely special about you, and that your date would be just as content with anyone so long as that individual had your height and hair color. In fact, there are millions of people with whom your date would be equally satisfied. Your heart would drop.

In addition to the disappointment, any preexisting fears of marriage would be exacerbated. Surely, you would also immediately dismiss this person as a serious marriage prospect and likely never see that individual again.

When interviewers ask why you want to become a part of their company, they are essentially asking you, "Why do you want to marry our organization?" If you are too general, they will respond in the same manner. Their heart will drop also, and they won't want to see you again either. Just like a date, they are hoping you are the *one*. When you're clearly not, they get disappointed too.

A more appropriate response to the marriage question might sound something like this:

SITUATION:

You are on a date, exploring the possibility of marriage.

YOUR QUESTION:

"So why do you want to marry me?"

APPROPRIATE RESPONSE:

"I want to marry you because of so many reasons! You're supportive, thoughtful, entirely devoted to me, and have a brilliant mind. You have a tremendous sense of humor, and you always know how to make me smile no matter what the situation. You genuinely care about my family and friends, and they all think the world of you. You're a terrific listener, and you're great with children. We both have similar views on raising a family, and you'll make a great parent. You are a brilliant writer, and I love to read. We both love jazz, traveling, and spending time together. The better question is, why *wouldn't* I want to marry you? You complete me. I can't see myself with anyone else."

RATIONALE:

In this example, you get an entirely different, much more positive impression (and feeling) when the person is more specific. Here, your date has specifically and positively described *you*—and only you—effectively and sincerely communicating that you are special, you are the one your date wants. You complement each other. The two of you are better together than either one alone. Your date's response also shows that he or she has paid attention to you, cared enough to learn specific things about you, and that your date is interested in you. As a result, your fears are diminished, you feel good and will not only want to see that person again, but can see how he or she will fit into your future. This more personalized and detailed response will have exactly the same effect on an interviewer. The interviewer will want to see you again too!

The following example demonstrates how this same principle applies to an interviewing situation.

SITUATION:

The *dating analogy* being applied to an interviewing situation.

INTERVIEWER'S QUESTION:

"So why are you seeking a career with our company?"

INAPPROPRIATE RESPONSE:

"Because you're a good company."

RATIONALE:

This response is much too general. There are thousands of "good" companies. There is nothing unique mentioned about the company and, therefore, offers the interviewer absolutely no assurance the candidate is truly interested in *their particular* company or that they would be a long-term fit. The candidate needs to be much more specific and substantive to be taken seriously.

APPROPRIATE RESPONSE:

"Because of many things. You are a Fortune 500 Company with an excellent reputation. You are the recognized leader in your field for innovations in technology. Despite a challenging economy, you have managed to sustain exceptional growth and were voted one of the top ten employers to work for. The commitment you have toward the advancement and development of your employees is remarkable. I, too, have been recognized in my field for leadership and technological innovations. My ideas have led to sustained growth in a highly competitive market. Like you, I am constantly striving to improve myself and my company. I couldn't think of another place I would prefer to work!"

RATIONALE:

This is a very specific, highly customized, and enthusiastic response. It shows the interviewer that the candidate cared enough to learn the unique aspects of their company and provides the interviewer assurance that the candidate specifically wants a position with *their* company and not just *any* company.

The above example demonstrates how simple it is to apply the *dating analogy* to an interviewing situation. By understanding how an employer feels (and more importantly, what that employer needs), you are able to move forward with them in the interview process versus being disqualified early on.

DETERMINING IDEAL RESPONSES

The *dating analogy* principle applies to virtually every aspect of the interview process, from preparation to job offer, from what you should wear to how to prepare. It applies to how you should present yourself and to what you should say or not say. Furthermore, it applies to physical aspects such as grooming and body language. Even facial expressions, posture, and eye contact can be correlated to this analogy.

Imagine that every time you looked up from your plate, your date was looking somewhere else. Or envision going to a black-tie affair, and your date shows up wearing shorts.

Remember, interviewers feel and respond the same way we do. Via the *dating analogy*, you can immediately see how important excellent eye contact and appropriate attire are on an interview.

The same principle applies when responding to an interviewer's questions.

To determine the ideal response on an interview, particularly when presented with a difficult question, simply ask yourself, "If this were a date and I had asked my date a similar question, what response would I need to feel comfortable or reassured?" Once you have determined the appropriate response on a date, you will have the answer on the interview, virtually every time! It's that easy.

This will be explored further in Chapter 4, "What Employers Are Looking For."

So if you ever find yourself in a pinch, uncertain of exactly what to do or not to do, what to say or not to say, just take a few seconds, relax, and reflect on this analogy. The appropriate response will come to you.

Keep this analogy in mind as you read through this book. It will help you to fully understand and appropriately respond to the unique underlying dynamics that exist with an interviewer and expertly navigate through the interviewing process.

THE SEVEN FUNDAMENTALS: WHAT EMPLOYERS ARE LOOKING FOR

REMEMBER THE DATING ANALOGY!

As with people in relationships, an employer evaluates you as a potential match based on several key criteria. In order to successfully progress through the interview process as well as to perform optimally on the job, it is truly essential you fully understand and meet these criteria. The bottom line is if you don't know exactly what someone expects, it's very difficult to provide it. So to avoid the guesswork and lay the groundwork for a successful interview, let's begin with what an employer is looking for. Keep in mind the *dating analogy*.

THE SEVEN FUNDAMENTALS

WHAT EMPLOYERS ARE LOOKING FOR

The following principles will guide you into the mind of the employer. They will give you an overview of precisely what the person sitting across the desk expects from you.

Although it reads like a laundry list, you can't skip any of these principles. They are inextricably linked. Know these, and you're off to an excellent start!

THE SEVEN FUNDAMENTALS YOU MUST HAVE:

1. Knowledge of what you want
2. A clear understanding of the job, the company, its products and/or services, and the industry
3. The necessary background, experience, and skill set
4. A high level of motivation and enthusiasm about the job
5. A positive attitude
6. The ability to clearly communicate all of the above
7. Compatibility with the interviewer and company

These *Seven Fundamentals* will be explained fully in the pages to come.

Prior to your interview, verify whether you meet all these requirements, (except Fundamental Rule #7, which will be determined when you meet the interviewer). If you don't meet these requirements, you are not ready yet. You should either continue on with your research and development until you do meet these requirements or re-evaluate whether the job you are seeking is the job for you.

FUNDAMENTAL RULE #1:
KNOWLEDGE OF WHAT YOU WANT

DO YOU KNOW WHAT YOU WANT?

If you've ever been involved with someone who didn't know what he or she wanted, you'll understand the frustration an interviewer feels when he or she comes across a candidate who is unsure. Interviewers don't have time to wait (or waste) while you're figuring things out, nor will they.

KNOW WHAT AND WHY

- One of the first questions most companies ask you is "Why us?" and if you're changing careers, "Why this industry?"
- You must be able to say *specifically* what you want, why you are interested in a particular company or industry, and how you are a perfect for it. To do so, you must know the details of the company. (Hint: Do your homework.)
- Be clear and consistent with your objectives.
- You must be focused and demonstrate a specific interest in one specific field versus several. (You may have multiple interests and skills, but it is essential that your stated objectives are in line with what the employer is offering.)

SITUATION:

Candidate interviewing for a health care sales position.

INTERVIEWER'S QUESTION:

"What are you looking for?"

INAPPROPRIATE RESPONSES:

1. "I'm looking for a challenge."
2. "I'm interested in a challenging career in either sales or marketing or teaching, and possibly starting my own business one day."

RATIONALE:

Similar to the example in "The Dating Analogy" chapter, both responses are too vague. With regard to response number 1, a person can get a challenge from rowing a boat. The candidate doesn't explain specifically what he is looking for. There are no clear, focused objectives. Consequently, the interviewer can have no confidence in the candidate's commitment to the industry, much less the company, and will not be inclined to proceed with that candidate. In example number 2, the candidate demonstrates a complete lack of focus and even suggests he may leave to start his own business one day. Think about how you would feel if your date told you up front, "I'm planning on leaving you someday." Short- and long-term goals must be aligned.

APPROPRIATE RESPONSE:

"I am specifically interested in a health care sales career where I can utilize my clinical background and interact with health care professionals. I want an environment where I can continuously learn, have opportunities for advancement, and be rewarded for my efforts. I also very much want to help to improve the quality of people's lives."

RATIONALE:

This response is much more specific and applies precisely to the health care sales profession, leaving the interviewer with no doubt about the candidate's interests, which are in line with the company's industry. Additionally, by mentioning an interest in "opportunities for advancement," the candidate also implies he plans to perform well and grow with the company, further increasing the interviewer's comfort with him from a long-term commitment standpoint.

So if an interviewer asks, "If you could do anything, what would it be?" or "Where do you see yourself in five years?" or any interest-related question, you should never express any desire you may have that is unrelated to the industry, company, or job at hand. Make sure your expression of what you want is what they have to offer.

DO THEY HAVE WHAT YOU WANT?

- Do your homework. Conduct research on the industry, company, and position.
- Before you decide to interview you should know, at least generally, whether the company and industry offers what you need and want. (This includes job responsibilities, company culture, compensation, etc.)
- Be realistic with your expectations and needs.
- Prepare and maintain an ongoing list of pros and cons.

DETERMINE YOUR SALARY REQUIREMENTS

- Know your value and salary requirements. Be realistic.
- Determine if the company's salary range and benefits package is acceptable to you prior to your first interview if possible. Make every effort to avoid waiting until an offer comes in.
- Settle on your minimum requirements and walk-away point up front.
- While most companies have some flexibility with their starting salaries, if the top of their range is significantly lower than the bottom of yours, you're probably setting yourself up for a disappointment. It's okay to aim for the high end of a range, just make sure your high is their high. If your requirements are significantly above the company's range, you may want to find a more suitable position or company.

(Generally recommend listing a salary *range* on any application forms whenever possible.)

- Keep in mind, stating unrealistic salary requirements can disqualify you.

FUNDAMENTAL RULE #2:
A CLEAR UNDERSTANDING OF THE JOB (THE COMPANY, ITS PRODUCTS, SERVICES, AND THE INDUSTRY)

DO YOU UNDERSTAND THE JOB?

There are several steps to thoroughly understanding a job and the responsibilities that go along with it. All are critical. The first one is doing your homework.

DO YOUR HOMEWORK!

Doing your homework is the foundation of any successful interview. You can't truly say, "I've got what it takes" if you don't know, specifically, what it takes. A climber doesn't set out to conquer Mt. Everest without first having a thorough understanding of what to expect on the journey, including determining weather conditions, understanding the challenges, evaluating his or her own strengths and limitations, surveying the terrain, preparing the necessary gear, etc. Similarly, you should never enter an interview without first thoroughly doing your research.

Imagine that, finally, your dream date says yes! This person is interested in going out with you. You surprise your date with a romantic seafood and jazz dinner cruise, only to find that your dream date is afraid of the water, allergic to seafood, and hates jazz. Your intentions were good. You just positioned yourself the wrong way. A little homework would have prevented this tragedy. A lot of homework and it could have been a picture-perfect evening. The most unfortunate part of this example is that it was totally avoidable. Remember, you can't step forward with any degree of certainty if you don't know what you're stepping into. So do your homework; be thorough so you know how to position yourself on an interview.

The more you learn about a company prior to your interview, the better. This knowledge allows you to clearly identify and explain how your attributes and the company's are mutually compatible, making you the ideal candidate. It also demonstrates to the interviewer that you have taken the time to learn about the company, its background, and interests, which shows you are serious about the opportunity. When employers know you care, they will take you more seriously as a candidate.

WHAT DOES "DOING YOUR HOMEWORK" LOOK LIKE?

Doing your homework goes well beyond the standard website research most people do. That would be similar to simply reading a book about Mt. Everest before attempting to climb it. While website research is certainly essential in that it provides a foundational understanding of the company, its vision, products, financials, and accomplishments, it is a fairly one-dimensional view. It doesn't necessarily tell you what it's like to actually work for the company on a day-to-day basis or some of the real-life challenges that exist. More thorough Internet searches on the company (beyond the website) can provide some very helpful supplemental information. A Google name search, for example, will provide a plethora of non company-sponsored information that will help broaden your understanding of the company, its products, services as well as competitors. If preparation time is limited, this Internet-website combination can be the best way to go.

An excellent means of gathering multidimensional information on a company is the good old-fashioned way; from its employees. Contact several to get their perspective on challenges, opportunities, culture, and day-to-day operations within their organization. Whether you find them through personal or professional referrals, internet sites such as Linked-In, direct contact with the company, or other means, real live people are your best bet. Ask detailed questions of as many people as possible but at least three if you can for a varied perspective.

Another outstanding source of information is a company's customers. Whereas employees may be somewhat reluctant to share certain things, customers have nothing to lose. If you were seeking a health care sales position for example, you should speak with doctors, pharmacists, and other health care personnel, even patients to gain their perspective on the company, its products, representatives, and competitors. Essentially, wherever the employees go or the products and services reach, you should go and ask questions.

You want to be very thorough when doing your homework. Remember, the more research you do, the greater your understanding. The greater your understanding, the more accurately and effectively you can explain how you fit into a company's environment and the better you will perform on your interview. (You can never do too much homework!)

THINGS TO THOROUGHLY FAMILIARIZE YOURSELF WITH

THE COMPANY

- Name of company, parent and sister companies (if any)
- Key leadership, including names, titles, tenure, accomplishments (if time allows)
- Mission and values
- History
- Recent news and/or accolades
- Day to day operations (what it's really like)
- Products and services (at least a basic familiarity and more as time permits)
- Proper pronunciation of all names, products, and services

COMPETITORS

- Names and standing of major competitors
- Products or services (if time allows)
- Advantages and disadvantages (if time allows)

CUSTOMERS

- Who they are
- Their thoughts about the industry
- Their thoughts about the company (pros and cons)
- Why they do or don't do business with the company
- How long they have done business with the company
- Their thoughts about the company's competitors, its employees, products, and services
- Speak to as many as possible (at least three) for a varied perspective

DOING YOUR HOMEWORK (BEYOND THE WEBSITE)

SITUATION: AN INDIVIDUAL SEEKING A HEALTH CARE SALES POSITION.

WHERE TO GO:

Any health care professional's place of business related to the product or service including physician offices, medical buildings, hospitals, pharmacies, clinics, urgent care centers, HMOs, etc.

WHO TO SEE:

Anyone and everyone affiliated with or impacted by the company or its products. This includes individuals at all levels of an organization ranging from office managers to nurses and physicians, to administrators, directors, and CEOs. It should also include even end-users of the company's products.

A FEW SAMPLE QUESTIONS TO ASK

- Are you familiar with (company's name)?
- How long have you been doing business/working with this company?
- Do you enjoy working with this company?
- What particular qualities do you like/dislike about this company, its employees, products, or services?
- How does this company's employees, product/service reputation compared to other companies/ industries?
- What are the key skill sets/traits of the more outstanding employees?
- Why do you use this company's products or services?
- What current or future challenges do you see for this company and why?
- What are your needs and does this company meet them? How?
- Do you feel this company offers strong growth opportunities for its employees?
- How is the quality of life of the employees?
- If you could design the ideal company for your needs, what would it look like?
- What would you like to see this company change?

You get the picture. Whatever the industry, ask, ask, ask.

THE BENEFITS OF DOING YOUR HOMEWORK

- Helps you to uncover important facts about the company, the position, the challenges and opportunities, providing you with a clear understanding of what to expect.
- Helps to determine how and if the position and the company suit you.
- Allows you to better position yourself as a "perfect fit." Once you are aware of the challenges and the environment, you can then explain how your background has prepared you to meet those challenges and excel in that environment.
- Shows the interviewer that he or she is worth your time and effort to gather information and that you went "above and beyond" to prepare, which demonstrates your sincere interest in and commitment to the position. (Key qualities employers are looking for).

AN ADDITIONAL NOTE ON HOMEWORK

Continue to do homework throughout the interview process. Following each interview, immediately research any key issues, details, or discussion points so that you are prepared to address them fully on any subsequent interviews. Be prepared and don't delay. You could be called back at any moment. Sharing your research findings will demonstrate to the interviewer your sense of urgency, excellent follow up skills, and a continued interest in the job. This will set you even further apart from your competition. As you uncover new details about the position or company, you may find they line up nicely with your background experience and skill set. Fundamental Rule #3 will walk you through how to inventory these strengths and blend them with the needs of the company and the position.

FUNDAMENTAL RULE #3: THE NECESSARY BACKGROUND, EXPERIENCE, AND SKILL SET

DO YOU UNDERSTAND YOUR OWN STRENGTHS?

As important as it is to do your homework on the company, it is equally critical you do your homework on yourself so that you know what you yourself have to offer.

DOING HOMEWORK ON YOURSELF

To get a job offer, you must convince and reassure the interviewer you are a picture-perfect fit for the position. To accomplish this, you must first thoroughly understand the job you're seeking. Then, you must identify your own strengths so that you can explain how you and your strengths fit perfectly into that picture. There is a simple yet essential exercise designed to help you do this extremely effectively: The *Greatest Strengths Worksheet*.

THE GREATEST STRENGTHS WORKSHEET / IDENTIFYING YOUR GREATEST STRENGTHS

If you had only ten minutes to prepare for an interview and could do only one thing, do this: Complete the *Greatest Strengths Worksheet*.

This exercise is probably *the single most important interview preparation step you can take*.

The *Greatest Strengths Worksheet* information, once completed, accounts for nearly 70 percent of what transpires on an interview. It allows you to address the three main things an employer wants to know. These three key elements are the following:

A) Who are you? (As defined by your greatest strengths)
B) Proof that you are who you say you are (via specific supportive examples of those strengths)
C) How you (and your strengths) correlate with the job requirements and benefit their company

That's it! Easy as A, B, C.

Very important: There are more details on the completion of the *Greatest Strengths Worksheet* at the end of this book in Section V.

Be absolutely sure to complete and review thoroughly the Greatest Strengths Worksheet as it is a quintessentially critical component of a successful interview.

Once you have familiarized yourself with your own skills and strengths, when you are challenged on an interview (which you will be), you can confidently and continuously reassure the interviewer that you are the ideal person for the job by sharing strength after strength, example after supportive example.

This exercise of completing the *Greatest Strengths Worksheet* will also help strengthen your courage muscle as you prepare for your interview. Upon completion, you will be able to see just clearly how much value you are actually bringing to the table. Just read what you have written about yourself! You will be amazed. It works!

WHAT CONSTITUTES A "GREATEST STRENGTH"?

A *Greatest Strength* is any attribute or skill set you have that is directly or indirectly related to the job and or company for which you are interviewing. In the eyes of an employer, your strengths define you, so your greatest strengths should be the best of the best of what you have to offer. Greatest strengths will vary depending on your experience and the type of position for which you are interviewing. Sales ability, leadership, communication skills, innovation, energy, customer service, technological expertise, clinical acumen, strategic partnering, financial management skills, creativity, tenacity, perseverance, being multilingual are just a few examples of greatest strengths. Examples, however, can be endless (more are listed in section 5, at the end of this book). For any given position, there are multiple examples you can use. The key is to be sure that your stated strengths align with the requirements of the position. If, for example, an individual with artistic talent were to apply for a sales position, unless there was some specific aspect of the job requiring creative art talent, *graphic design* shouldn't be included as one of the greatest strengths as it is not relevant.

By contrast, if a business executive were applying for a corporate management position, that individual might site leadership, communication skills, strategic planning, collaboration, financial management, tenacity, and perseverance as some of his or her greatest strengths. It is important to have a sufficient quantity of salient strengths that align with the needs of the job at hand.

DO YOU HAVE RECENT TANGIBLE EXAMPLES THAT SUPPORT EVERYTHING YOU CLAIM?

Always provide specific tangible examples.

Companies invest a great deal of time and money into their employees and need to be assured you can do what is required of you to perform optimally in the position. Articulating your greatest strengths is a critical part of that. Simply claiming you have a given strength, however, is not enough since anyone can make a claim. You also must have specific supportive examples to back up your claims.

If you say you can do something, you must prove it. If you say you have certain experience, you must describe it. Think of this proof as the collateral required to substantiate your claims. Always be prepared to tie-in examples and accomplishments from work or life-related experiences to prove who you are. *Always.* And you must provide these specific, tangible examples for every claim you make about yourself automatically, even if the interviewer does not specifically ask. It is imperative you share this supportive information.

Be proactive. The more proof you provide, the greater the employer's reassurance. The greater their reassurance, the less fear and doubt they feel and the more likely you are to progress through the interview process (see the *Greatest Strengths Worksheet*).

A FEW KEY POINTERS ON PROVIDING PROOF (SUPPORTIVE EXAMPLES)

- Don't wait for the interviewer to ask. (When describing a strength, automatically link the supportive example with that strength.)
- Avoid using hypothetical examples (even when responding to hypothetical questions).
- Hypothetical responses provide no proof.
- If you are presented with a hypothetical situation, tie your answer in to a similar, real-life situation

you have been through. This will give you the proof source you need for a credible response.

- The majority of your examples should be recent work-related examples.
- It is important to demonstrate a consistent history of excellent performance, so in addition to citing recent supportive examples, occasionally (but to a lesser extent) cite more distant examples as well.

WHAT CONSTITUTES A "TANGIBLE EXAMPLE" (OR PROOF SOURCE)?

- A specific and detailed explanation (be prepared to provide names, dates, locations, numbers, etc.)
- Physical documentation, such as:
  - Awards and/or honors received
  - Tracking data and/or reports
  - Verbal and/or written confirmation from an authorized credible source (i.e. an immediate supervisor, president and/or CEO, upper division management, significant customer, etc.)
  - Performance evaluations
  - Photos

THE "PAST BEHAVIOR" RULE

The Past Behavior Rule is simply this: past behavior is an excellent predictor of future behavior and behavior itself is an excellent predictor of success.

Interviewers follow this very basic but profound principle when screening candidates. Simply put, interviewers ask questions about your past to determine who you are and how you will perform in the future if you're hired. That is, they're seeking to determine your future likelihood of success or failure based on your past performance. It is a very accurate indicator: if you were a top performer in the past, you are likely to be a top performer in the future; if you managed your time well in the past, you are likely to manage your time well in the future; and so on.

Conversely, if you failed to fulfill your obligations or frequently changed jobs in the past, you are likely to do the same in the future (often, regardless of your "reasons" for doing so). Therefore, always be prepared to present, illustrate, and tie-in previous experiences, strengths, and accomplishments that positively support who you are and how you will perform in the future.

HELPFUL TIPS

- Imagine that the position you are applying for is like a puzzle requiring all the necessary pieces to be perfectly complete.
- Think of all your experiences as the various pieces to that puzzle.
- When you put the pieces all together, you have everything the position requires.

- On your interview, simply describe the pieces you are bringing to the table.
- Refer to your specific, related examples of past behavior, experiences, and accomplishments.
- Tie in these experiences with those qualifications the employer is seeking, explaining how those pieces—when put together, perfectly complete the puzzle—demonstrating you have everything the position requires!
- Be sure to complete the *Greatest Strengths Worksheet* in Section V, at the end of this book.

EXPLAINING JOB CHANGES

Similar to a person interested in settling down, employers want security and reassurance. You must make them feel secure in your stability before they will be comfortable moving you forward in the interview process. Frequent job changes can generate interviewer doubts and uncertainty as you can be perceived as a flight risk.

The bottom line is this: with the exception of corporate downsizing, most job changes are based on decisions you have made. Good or bad, they are a direct reflection of you, your thought process, and the perceived stability (or instability) you will bring to a future job. (Remember the past behavior rule.) Therefore, you must carefully explain the rationale behind your decisions, demonstrate good judgment, and assure the interviewer that you are not a flight risk. You made the decision to do your research or not, accept the job, and then to leave the job—unless you were asked to, which is a different story entirely.

Employers want people who take responsibility for their actions and make good business decisions, not someone who blames the situation. Solid decisions require planning, research, and thought. Similar to a relationship (the *dating analogy*), people often claim "surprises" that appear over time as the reasons for leaving. "I didn't know it was going to be like this (or that)…and that's why I'm leaving." Leaving a position (or any relationship) earlier than expected generally just indicates that the person didn't do enough preplanning, research, or enough thought to the decision to accept the responsibility in the first place. "Why *didn't* you know?" is the question. If you do find yourself in such a situation, you must be able to explain that you have learned from your past mistakes, instead of trying to blame the company or the situation since your new employer doesn't want similar "surprises" to be the reason for your leaving them.

BREAKING THE PATTERN

If your job history (past behavior) consists of a string of frequent changes, you must show the interviewer you have taken ownership of your choices and that you have grown from your past decisions. You must reassure them that you have learned how to prevent repeating this pattern going forward. To do this, make sure you do your homework thoroughly on the new prospective company. Learn what questions to ask, particularly those you may have overlooked with your previous positions so you don't run into the same "surprises."

WHAT *NOT TO DO* WHEN EXPLAINING JOB CHANGES

Except in corporate downsizing situations

- Blame the situation
- Blame your employer
- Blame "on the job" surprises that came up
- Claim you "didn't know this" or "didn't know that"

WHAT YOU *SHOULD DO* WHEN EXPLAINING JOB CHANGES

- Acknowledge your role in the situation, (similar to a relationship, if you chose it, take ownership of it).
- In situations where a "surprise" caused you to leave, explain how you've learned to ask the right preliminary questions to avoid that or similar surprises in the future.
- Explain how you have more thoroughly researched this particular position and industry than you had previously and describe how you have made every possible effort to avoid any future surprises. (Make sure you have!)
- Explain any deliberate stepping stone positions (i.e., that you accepted a particular position so that

you could gain the necessary experience to prepare you for your new career). This demonstrates a well thought-out plan or strategy.

EXPLAINING THE PAST: POOR CHOICES OR GETTING FIRED

- Interviewers' systematic array of questions are designed to uncover the truth. Overall, they are very effective.
- Save yourself the hassle, anxiety, doubt, and embarrassment and tell the truth from the beginning about everything (GPA, driving and credit record, past employment, etc.).
- Misinformation often becomes quite transparent over time. Employers appreciate honesty. So if you've made a mistake or a poor decision in the past that surfaces during an interview, explain what you've learned from it and how you have built upon the experience and strengthened who you are today. Be sure to provide specific examples to support your claim.

DON'T JUMP SHIP TOO SOON!

- If possible, remain in your current position until you have secured a new one.
- Interviewers are naturally skeptical (and have to be to protect themselves). Remaining employed during your job search will help avoid raising interviewer

concerns or "red flags" that you were fired, about to be fired, exercised poor judgment, or that you are independently wealthy (and don't really need a job).

FUNDAMENTAL RULE #4: A HIGH LEVEL OF MOTIVATION AND ENTHUSIASM ABOUT THE JOB

DO YOU HAVE THE NECESSARY MOTIVATION?

Companies want "hungry" individuals, not just experienced ones. You must express your enthusiasm and interest clearly (both verbally and nonverbally). You must convey that you are "on fire" for the job, as one manager so aptly put it. Tell the interviewer specifically what excites you about the position. Upon completion of your homework, you should find there is plenty to be excited about. When demonstrating your enthusiasm, be sure to share only those things that you are truly interested in and excited about. In other words, don't fake it. Your level of sincerity (or insincerity) will be transparent to the interviewer. It is critical you come across as genuine. Think of the *dating analogy* parallel: you are listening to someone say all the right things, but you don't believe a word of it. The person is unemotional, unconvincing, and dry. How many dates follow versus when you genuinely feel the person is being sincere?

Sincere enthusiasm is a proactive energy that can and should be expressed in a multitude of ways. Interviewers need to see it too.

The following are two key things to remember.

1. GIVE EVERY INTERVIEW 100 PERCENT

- Give every interview everything you've got! (This can make the difference between an average interview and an excellent one.)
- Apply the *dating analogy* principle.
- Show the same level of excitement and energy for the position as you would for things in life that would excite you most: winning a trip, meeting a favorite celebrity, an all-you-can-eat buffet filled with your favorite desserts, etc.
- Maintain this level of enthusiasm and interest throughout the interview process. Make no exceptions.
- Don't slouch, give up, stop smiling, or so much as think anything inappropriate while you are still in view or earshot of an interviewer or their colleagues. (And remember your interview isn't over until you have left the premises.)
- A position isn't yours until you have a signed offer letter. Don't slow down or slack off.
- *Important Note*: If you ever decide a job may not be an ideal fit, you can always withdraw, but do so *in-between* interviews, never *during* an interview. Never give less than 100 percent during an interview. If you do, the interviewer will make the decision

for you, at which point, even if you change your mind, it is too late. If doubts should arise during an interview, don't show them. (Quite often doubts are clarified later.) Doubts in you often become transparent and trigger doubts in an interviewer. Keep the decision in your hands. If you do have doubts, you can ask questions for clarification, but always ask with interest and enthusiasm. This way you are able to gather information that will help you make a decision without triggering doubts in the interviewer's mind.

2. MAKE IT A PRIORITY!

Make everything about your interviewing a priority. Be prepared. Begin your homework immediately. Return calls promptly. Virtually, nothing should come between you and an interview at your target company. If you are currently employed, taking a personal or vacation day is highly recommended so that no unforeseen circumstances come up. Plus, it will ease your nerves, and you can focus completely on your interview. Second chances and rescheduling are often not an option, so jump through whatever hoops you must to get there (with a smile) and show the interviewer you're serious about them. If you allow other things to interfere (even if you are under the weather), you risk giving the impression that the new job isn't important enough to you. Get it right the first time! Avoid regrets. (Many of us can easily apply the *dating analogy* here!)

TWO ACCEPTABLE EXCUSES FOR BEING LATE OR MISSING AN INTERVIEW

There are two acceptable excuses for being late for or missing an interview—a wedding or a funeral (both your own). In other words, don't be late, don't reschedule, and don't let anything come between you and your interview!

FUNDAMENTAL RULE #5: A POSITIVE ATTITUDE

The difference between success and failure is far more often attitude than ability.

STAY POSITIVE!

It is absolutely critical that you maintain a positive attitude about yourself, your experiences, and others throughout the interview process. You will be faced with a multitude of "trick" questions and scenarios all designed to get you to share negative things about yourself. Don't be fooled. No matter how many times you are pressed to do so, no matter what the temptation, stay positive.

IMPORTANCE OF STAYING POSITIVE

Understand that the interviewer's job is to uncover anything that may prevent you from doing an exemplary job in their company. Your job on the other hand is to present yourself as a picture-perfect fit for the position, reassure the interviewer, and dispel any and all notions to the contrary. Not some. Not most. *All*.

NEVER SAY ANYTHING NEGATIVE ABOUT YOURSELF!

The impression an interviewer forms is like a snapshot in time. The interviewer will make a decision to move forward or not based on that snapshot. Since employers are seeking a perfect match, not an "okay" match or even a "good" one, you must present your snapshot as *perfect*. Admitting flaws or giving in to any form of negativity is essentially like blemishing your own snapshot.

Plain and simple, *never say or acknowledge anything negative about yourself!*

Nor should you confirm a negative statement or drawback made by an interviewer, ever. When you're challenged to make such a confession, simply don't. Instead, assertively, positively, and pleasantly turn it around.

If for example, an interviewer thinks you lack experience in a given area, there is no need to get defensive or feel defeated, simply explain to them what experience you *do have*, tying in specific examples of related experiences and skill sets that support your effort. The specific, tangible examples help minimize or eliminate the perceived drawback.

Believe in yourself wholeheartedly and you will rise up to the challenges you will face. Keep your snapshot clean and perfect. Remember this rule. Live by it and you will be way ahead in the interview game.

Following is an example.

SITUATION:

A recent graduate being interviewed for a sales position.

INTERVIEWER'S COMMENT:

"Sarah, you interview well, and I like you. It's just too bad you don't have any sales experience." (A negative statement about the candidate's experience..)

INAPPROPRIATE RESPONSE:

"I know, but can you give me a chance?"

RATIONALE:

The interviewer is challenging the candidate with a negative, saying, "It's just too bad you don't have any sales experience." When the candidate says, "I know, but...," she is breaking the rule to *stay positive* by acknowledging the negative and admitting that she is not a perfect fit, which allows interviewer doubt into the picture. Now, the only option is to hope for mercy from the interviewer (not an optimal position to be in on an interview).

APPROPRIATE RESPONSE:

"Well, let me share with you how I actually *do* have the sales experience you are seeking. For example, in school I developed a major networking initiative that allowed students from different areas of study to collaborate, share ideas, and learn from each other. I had to sell the idea, not only to the other students, but also to my professor and the dean. It took an entire semester to get the necessary buy-in from the students and faculty, but eventually, my concept was accepted and it is still in place today."

RATIONALE:

In this response, the candidate never acknowledged the negative. Instead, she provided a specific, tangible example showing how she had *exactly* what the interviewer was looking for.

In the above example, the candidate is simply being tested by the interviewer. As you can see with her appropriate response, this individual passed the test with flying colors. Remember, the company knew the candidate's experience before she arrived, and she was still invited to interview, which means the minimum requirements on paper were already met. So when you're confronted with a similar situation, don't doubt yourself. Instead, when you're challenged, remain calm, positive, and rise up to the challenge with supportive examples!

GIVE YOURSELF THE BENEFIT OF THE DOUBT!

- Always give yourself the benefit of the doubt throughout the interview process.
- Deliberately maintain your optimism throughout the interview process.
- Your attitude and belief will positively (or negatively) affect how you handle yourself and how interviewers will perceive you.
- Unless you've gotten a "Dear John" letter or a call saying otherwise, you're still in the game, so stay positive. You'll be (pleasantly) surprised at the difference it makes.

SUCCESS AND STRESS-RELIEF SECRET

When you're on an interview, particularly with a difficult to read, stone-faced interviewer where staying positive can be a challenge because you don't know what the interviewer is thinking, repeat this silently to yourself: *"This interviewer loves me, loved that answer, and is eating this up!"*

This does several key things. In an otherwise potentially stressful situation, it will make you smile and relax. As you lighten up a bit, you will have more energy to feel and stay positive. The more positive you are, the more the interviewer will like and respond favorably to you. Plus and most importantly, you'll often be right, the interviewer *will* love you!

TURNING "WEAKNESSES" AND "LIMITATIONS" INTO POSITIVES

"What's your greatest weakness?"

"Where have you tried your best but failed?"

These are two commonly asked questions that are, more often than not, mishandled by even the most experienced interviewees.

Responding appropriately to questions regarding weaknesses and shortcomings is essential to maintaining a positive and credible impression with an interviewer. Many candidates have unknowingly disqualified themselves with their responses to these and similar questions. They inadvertently say something that is genuinely negative about themselves that can leave an indelible stain on their qualifications in the eye of an interviewer. After all, *no employer* wants to hire someone that is weak. Remember, you want to be a positive and a "perfect fit." You don't want to air all of your flaws or even a few. So how do you respond positively to a direct question asking you to share something negative about yourself in a candid and credible manner?

Easy. First and foremost, change your mind-set. Think of a *weakness* as "a special desire or fondness" (Webster) or as something you can't turn off instead of a flaw. Weaknesses don't have to be bad. For example, a parent's weakness may be their children. What child wouldn't want that person as a parent? On your interview, you want to link your "weakness" to the needs of the employer. How do you accomplish this while being 100 percent sure you are not saying anything negative about yourself in the process by mistake?

Simple. Rather than answering negatively, share one of your greatest strengths instead: one that you are passionately obsessive about; one that you can't turn off, stop doing, or separate yourself from even if you wanted to. Describe that inability to stop exhibiting the strength as your "weakness."

For example, let's say you are the top-ranked sales manager in your division, and you have an insatiable drive to remain number one. You are miserable if you ever slip to number two and will go to great lengths to maintain your top ranking, going well above the job requirements, regularly putting in fifty, sixty, seventy hours a week to stay ahead of your colleagues.

Clearly, you are extremely driven. Being extremely driven is a greatest strength. The weakness is that you can't turn off that insatiable desire. You are "weak" to it, and as a result of that weakness, you continually strive to work harder and harder to maintain and improve your standing. If an employer were to ask, "What's your greatest weakness?" You might respond, "I have an insatiable desire to be number one" and, then, describe what that looks like.

In this example, the very thing you can't turn off is exactly what the employer is looking for, a highly driven employee! This is essential in any job that is goal or task oriented.

Be sure to complete and refer to your *Greatest Strengths Worksheet* in Section IV, Chapter 3.

EVEN WEAKNESSES AND LIMITATIONS MUST BE PRESENTED POSITIVELY

- If you do not possess a particular requirement, minimize the drawback by describing an alternate, even greater, related skill or strength that you *do have* to offer. Avoid acknowledging what you don't have.
- In the event an interviewer is outright mistaken about a drawback or weakness, simply and politely correct them saying, ""Let me explain how I actually do have (xyz)," and provide supportive examples.
- Remember the rule to *stay positive*! Never say anything negative about yourself. Ever.
- Turn every "weakness" into a positive.

SITUATION:

Interviewer exploring a candidate's weaknesses and limitations.

INTERVIEWER:

"What's your greatest weakness?"

INAPPROPRIATE RESPONSES:

1. "I tend to get very frustrated when things don't work out my way."
2. "I'm disorganized."

RATIONALE:

These responses dead-end with the problem. They offer no solutions, are entirely negative, and reflect true drawbacks. They fail to put the candidate in a positive light, leaving the interviewer with a negative impression.

APPROPRIATE RESPONSES:

1. "Despite winning the President's Club Award and exceeding my manager's expectations, *I'm never satisfied with my performance* and always want to have achieved more than I have, and I want it done yesterday."
2. "E-mail. I'm constantly checking it. *I can't stand being disorganized or falling behind*, so I've set up a system (past tense) where I prioritize messages by A, B, and C, and I'm able to complete all of my top tasks and RSVPs daily."
3. "*My customers.* There's nothing I wouldn't do to take care of them."

RATIONALE:

- In example number 1, the candidate's weakness is that they can't turn off their insatiable drive to continually improve even though they are already at the top. They are "never satisfied," even with exceptional performance. The result is an outstanding work ethic and ability to set and achieve extremely high goals. This candidate will always push to do more. A "weakness" every manager wants!
- In example number 2, because of the weakness, a disdain for disorganization, the candidate demonstrates exceptional organizational skills and the ability to get top priorities completed on time—a manager's dream.
- In example number 3, what employer wouldn't want their employee to go the extra mile for their customers? This, too, is a "weakness" the employer will benefit from.

ADDITIONAL NOTE ON WEAKNESSES:

You never want to say, "I'm *too* (this)" or "I'm *too* (that)" when responding to queries about your greatest weakness because anytime you are *too* anything; it really is a negative. Avoid this adverb.

The bottom line is that you want your weaknesses to be something the interviewer finds invaluable. It needs to be something that is an asset to the organization and the position. As described in the example above, a person being interviewed for a sales or service position whose greatest weakness is an undying passion for his or her customers, might state, "There is nothing I wouldn't do for them." This shows a hiring manager the candidate will go the extra mile for their clients. What manager doesn't want a representative with that mindset?

> Remember, "What's your greatest weakness?" is a trick question. It's not an opportunity to spill out all of your flaws, or even one, for that matter. Rather, it is an opportunity to demonstrate your greatest strengths and why you are the best person for the job. So before you respond to these frequently asked, important, and tricky questions, carefully evaluate your planned response. If there is so much as one negative word or thought in it, you need to modify that response.

RESPONDING TO QUERIES ABOUT PAST FAILURES

"Where have you tried your best but failed?" is another common interview question many interviewees are faced with. Answering this type of question without being negative can at first appear tricky. Knowing that you must stay positive and that an interviewer will use any information you share about your past behaviors as predictors of your future success (the Past Behavior Rule) can be somewhat disquieting.

But, again, there is a simple solution.

In fact, there are two ways of effectively responding to inquiries about failures.

OPTION 1:

Provide an example where your "failure" is better than other peoples' success in the same area. In other words, it's not really a failure at all—or at least not in the eyes of other people, but rather a success. For example, if an Olympic athlete who just won the Gold were asked where she had tried her best but failed responded by saying, "I failed to do my personal best. I know I could have finished three tenths of a second faster." This individual is showing that her standards are so exceptionally high, that despite being the best in the world, she wanted to do better. A sales representative might use an example where he won the top award, but still wanted to close one more account. A scientist may be recognized with an ingenious new discovery that saved millions of lives earning the Nobel Peace Prize, but he wished he had discovered it sooner. Each of these self-proclaimed failures are better than most peoples' greatest successes. We all have our own individual examples to share and these are what employers are seeking.

OPTION 2:

Share a true failure, but cite one that happened in the distant past where, as a result of that failure, you developed one of your greatest strengths. You must clearly demonstrate how you have learned and grown from the experience, incorporated the lesson into your life, and became a better, stronger, more effective person as a result. In other words, the failure itself led to your success.

If, for example, Arnold Schwarzenegger had been a skinny little kid unable to lift fifty pounds in a high school weight-lifting competition and decided that as a result of that failure that he would never fail again, secured a trainer, started working out seven days a week, and as a result became *the* Arnold Schwarzenegger, world-renowned body building champion, that would be an example of a failure leading to a greatest strength. The failure motivated him to succeed. If he hadn't failed, he might never have developed the strength. Utilize this type of example on your interview— just make sure it is related to your particular field of interest and linked to your own experiences and strengths.

The purpose of citing examples from the more distant past is because it often takes time to turn things around. Professional body builders don't morph over night, nor do any of us truly change that quickly. Enough time must have elapsed for the interviewer to be fully comfortable that the failure has led to a legitimate and permanent strength. If you share a failure that happened too recently, the interviewer may not be convinced you have had enough time to have truly learned or grown from the experience and is not going to want to gamble on the possibility that you haven't gotten it right yet.

SITUATION:

Candidate responses to a negative question.

INTERVIEWER'S QUESTION:

"Give me an example of when have you have tried your best, but failed."

INAPPROPRIATE RESPONSE:

"I had a project deadline to complete. The deadline was unrealistic, and despite my efforts, I didn't get it in on time. It really wasn't my fault."

RATIONALE:

This response fails to state anything positive. It not only blames the situation, but it is a true failure and makes the candidate look bad. This type of response could disqualify you.

APPROPRIATE RESPONSES:

My manager's goal was for me to close 50 percent of my ten target accounts last year. My personal goal was to close 100 percent. I successfully closed 90 percent, but failed to capture the last one. Although, I earned the region's top sales award for the accomplishment, I wasn't fully satisfied because I didn't close them all last year. This year, after many more months of effort, I finally landed the account. So now I can call it a true success."

RATIONALE:

This response shows that the candidate is an overachiever who sets and achieves very high goals. The candidate's "failure" is still better than the manager's expectations, earning the candidate a top regional award. The interviewer is left with a very positive impression.

NEVER SAY ANYTHING NEGATIVE ABOUT ANYONE ELSE

The rule to have a positive attitude crosses all categories. Whatever words leave your mouth must be constructive and edifying if you want a positive result. This holds true, whether you are speaking about a situation, a place, yourself, or someone else. All of it is a reflection on you.

Note the following example:

SITUATION:

Interviewer asking a negative question about someone else.

INTERVIEWER'S QUESTION:

"Have you ever worked for a manager you didn't like?"

INAPPROPRIATE RESPONSE:

"Yes, an awful one! He never got back to me on time, which was extremely frustrating. He was new and incompetent. He didn't know how to manage our business unit. Nobody liked him, and he was very difficult to work with."

RATIONALE:

The candidate breaks the rule of keeping a positive attitude. The candidate expresses feelings and opinions that are negative, bitter, and offers no solutions, only problems. In the interviewer's eyes, this negative attitude is actually an equally negative reflection on the candidate.

APPROPRIATE RESPONSE:

"When our manager was new, he had his hands full with a large district and a lot of responsibility. He wasn't always able to get back to us as quickly as we might have liked sometimes, so I learned how to become more resourceful and get the important information I needed to continue to perform optimally in my territory."

RATIONALE:

In this example, the candidate states facts without negativity, judgment, or bitterness and demonstrates the ability to respond favorably and develop a positive solution in the midst of a challenging situation. It is not about bashing and trashing, but, instead, showing how to handle oneself effectively and maintain a positive attitude toward the situation and others when difficulties arise. This will have a tremendously positive impression on an interviewer.

BE A PROBLEM SOLVER

No one likes complainers. When challenged to discuss a difficult or negative situation or experience, focus on your role in the situation, and how the outcome was positively changed as a direct or indirect result of your being involved. Show how you maintained a positive attitude about the situation, no matter how difficult. Never focus on the problem. Never present a problem without a solution.

REMEMBER, YOU'VE GOT WHAT IT TAKES!

- Visualize that you've already gotten the job, and now, you are simply explaining why you belong in the position.
- Think of the interview as a challenge for which you have all the skills to overcome, not an insurmountable object. Then, simply rise to the challenge.
- Take time to complete and review the *Greatest Strengths Worksheet*! Continually add to it. You will see just exactly how much you have to offer and why the company will be fortunate to have *you* in the new position!

STAY POSITIVE SUMMARY

- Never say anything negative about yourself or others.
- Never say anything negative. Period.

- If discussing something that has potentially negative or challenging aspects to it, be sure the last words out of your mouth regarding that issue are positive and/or solution-oriented. Never leave the interviewer with a negative. Never.

FUNDAMENTAL RULE #6: ABILITY TO COMMUNICATE EFFECTIVELY

CAN YOU COMMUNICATE YOUR FUNDAMENTAL QUALITIES?

DEVELOPING TRUST

Sincerity is a breeding ground for open communication. Don't pretend to be something or someone you're not. Never misrepresent yourself, and you will never have to worry later about being consistent or remembering what you said. Interviewing is an opportunity for two individuals to determine (truthfully and accurately) if they can mutually benefit one another. (Just like a date, if you misrepresent, you pay for it later.) There's a job out there for everyone; a stretch-goal is great, but if you have to stretch the truth, this may not be the job for you.

As mentioned previously, when explaining why you desire the position you are being interviewed for, be sure to only express those things that are truly interesting to you. This genuine expression of interest is essential. You can talk about these things endlessly and with passion. Don't just say what you think the interviewer wants to hear. For example, if the company's profit and loss statement is of no concern to you, don't provide that as one of the reasons you are interested. There should be enough other positive things that you are sincerely interested in that you can discuss. If you have to start making things up, you should probably reconsider the position and/or company.

PAY ATTENTION!

Actively listen. Read the interviewer's body language. Respond appropriately. Also, be sure to take notes. Besides being helpful to you, doing so communicates interest.

KEEP IT SIMPLE!

You must make communication as simple as possible. Everything from your résumé to ways to reach you (see "Pre-Interview Preparation," Section II, Chapters 1 and 2). If employers have to plow through too much on your résumé, they won't read it. If there's insufficient contact information, they won't contact you. If you ramble, they won't listen. Always be concise and direct.

TIE IT TOGETHER!

Put the pieces together for the interviewer. Explain exactly how and why you are a perfect match for the position. Don't assume interviewers automatically "see" how you fit in with their company. The *Greatest Strengths Worksheet* offers an easy A, B, C approach to doing so.

FUNDAMENTAL RULE #7: COMPATIBILITY WITH THE INTERVIEWER

ARE YOU COMPATIBLE?

While a personality match can never be guaranteed, there are a few things you can do to increase the likelihood of a positive connection. Begin with following fundamental rules 1 through 6 since interviewers tend to look more favorably upon individuals who meet those criteria. A few more suggestions are listed below:

- Mirror the interviewer. (If the interviewer talks very slowly, you should slow down a little and vice versa.)
- Listen actively.
- Read and respond appropriately to the interviewer's verbal and nonverbal cues.
- Respect the interviewer's time.
- Use the interviewer's name periodically.
- Pay attention to your intuition and respond accordingly.
- Don't forget to smile periodically.

If the interviewer is also the hiring manager, you generally can't lose, regardless of the outcome of your interview. Either way, it works out for the best. While of course you want to take the preliminary steps recommended above, the bottom line is if your personalities match, that's terrific and can lead to a gratifying, long-term working relationship. If they don't, that's okay too because you have found out early this is probably not someone you would want to work for in the first place. As difficult as it may be to hear, it is a win-win.

There is an exception you should be cognizant of. In the event the interviewer is not the hiring manager, but rather one of several people you meet throughout the interview process, you will want to do whatever you can to relate to them on their level, regardless of how challenging this may be. This is because this interviewer's personality does not necessarily reflect that of the company or the hiring manager, and you don't want to give up on a good opportunity because of a bad interviewer.

Now that you know what employers are looking for, it is time to show you the critical next steps: How to expertly prepare to present the absolute best of who you are to your future employer!

SECTION II

PRE-INTERVIEW PREPARATION

RÉSUMÉ TIPS

While the focus of this book is not on résumé writing, in this chapter you will find some key concepts and tips to help you prepare.

RÉSUMÉ TIPS

Think of fishing. Whether you're fishing for fish, fishing for a mate, or fishing for a job, the same principle applies. You must have the right lure. Without the right lure, despite there being plenty of fish in the sea, not only will you fail to catch the specific type of fish you are seeking, but you may fail to catch *any* fish whatsoever.

In this instance, your résumé is the lure. It's what gets the initial glance. Then, it will either attract, repel, or get no response at all. Similar to an encounter with a potential mate, there has to be some appeal to get any attention. Therefore, your résumé must have the features and ingredients necessary to attract the type of employers you are looking for.

Keep in mind, a lure only serves to attract the type of fish you want; it is the skill of the fisherman that lands the fish.

RÉSUMÉ RECOMMENDATIONS

APPEARANCE AND FORMAT

- Professional-style format. Appearance is important. Get it done professionally if necessary.
- Stay fairly conservative with your font and format.
- Avoid script and the old typewriter font for example, which is outdated and may give a less professional impression.
- Avoid darker résumé paper or paper with designs or pictures. Should an employer need to make copies, they don't reproduce well, plus the person reviewing your résumé may not have your same artistic taste. Such artistic accents can also be a distraction. It is best you stay neutral: white or a light beige. When in doubt, always err on the conservative side.
- Make sure the layout is consistent throughout (e.g., spacing, dates, job descriptions).
- Make sure all dates are accurate.
- Always spell-check, then double check, then recheck *manually*. There can be no grammatical or typographikal errors. (See how a tiny mistake stands out? *Typographical* was deliberately misspelled, in

case you missed it). Automatic spell-checking does not always catch grammatical or typographical errors, so you must also visually inspect.

CONTENT

- Include a clear, concise goal or objective, leaving no room for doubt as to what you are seeking. (Remember the *dating analogy*: be specific. This is particularly important when you are changing fields or if you have a widely varied background.)
- Name, address, and contact information (including phone and e-mail) should be at the top of the page in a larger font.
- Suggest a minimum size 14 font (or larger) for contact information to minimize risk of illegibility should a résumé be duplicated or faxed. (If employers can't read your information, they can't contact you.)
- Keep it simple.
- Keep to a maximum of two pages or, if possible, one. If you have additional important information to share, add a separate "Highlights" or "Summary" page. (Remember, the résumé is the lure. It's designed just to give employers a tasty bite, not fill them up with a ten-course meal).
- Avoid extensive text. The easier to read the better. Companies often receive hundreds of résumés for

a single position. Cluttered or complicated résumés simply take too much time to read and, as a consequence, are often not read at all. Additionally, important data tends to get "lost" in the text. Text should be in brief, easy-to-read bullet points where possible.

- Employment should be listed in reverse chronological order (beginning with your current or most recent position and working your way back).
- Always include current position.
- Avoid time gaps whenever possible. If you do have any, make sure they are accounted for.
- A cover letter can be used to explain significant time gaps, frequent job changes or layoffs.
- Education normally goes last. If, however, your education enhances your objective and your experience is light, it should appear immediately after your objective, prior to work experience. (For example, if you are seeking a medical or scientific sales position, have no sales experience, but have a background in biochemistry, don't bury this information at the end of your résumé.)
- All related significant accomplishments (e.g., awards, honors, or promotions) should be clearly noted. Bullet point format is excellent for quick, easy-to-read highlights.

- When describing job functions, include key words and responsibilities related to your objective. This can include descriptions of strengths, industry-specific skills and achievements.
- Incorporate action words, such as *achieved*, *designed*, *initiated*, *produced*, *developed*, *established*, *built*, *founded*, *implemented*, *recognized*, *elected*, and so forth to describe your activities.

OTHER KEY POINTERS

- Know your résumé. Study it. Be able to explain everything from start and end dates to job choices and employment gaps. (It can be very embarrassing when an interviewer knows your résumé better than you do.)
- If you can't explain it, don't include it.
- Accuracy is critical. If you don't pay attention to detail on your résumé, an employer will assume that you won't on the job either. (Hint: They're usually correct.)
- Avoid posting résumés as "confidential" on the Internet. Confidential résumés are highly impersonal and require significantly more time and effort to track than résumés with all the necessary contact and employer information listed. Remember, your goal is to make it easy for

employers to reach you and know about you. If it's too difficult, they will find someone else.

WHAT ABOUT FOLLOW UP?

One of the most common questions people have after submitting a résumé is, "When should I follow up?" As a general rule of thumb, use the following guidelines:

- Utilize polite persistence. If you have a contact at the company, you may call or e-mail once a résumé has been submitted to confirm receipt. Afterwards, follow up every two weeks to a month until you secure an interview. Avoid repeated, obsessive calling or e-mailing. Your goal is simply to convey to the would-be interviewer your interest, not to rush or bombard them, which can have negative effects.

- Often when applying to a company on line or via a job site, there is no single individual to follow up with. In these instances, you will generally receive a confirmation e-mail acknowledging receipt. Wait for additional contact from the employer. Do not submit multiple times for the same position. Someone is generally looking at these on the other end and repeated submissions can be perceived as an annoyance. Think of the *dating analogy*. Persistence is good. Obsession is not.

VOICE MAIL, PHONE, AND INTERNET TIPS

When a hiring manager receives an impressive résumé, that manager will often call the candidate immediately. If a manager were to call and get a voice mail with singing, laughing, or a five-minute song, he or she will probably hang up. Be prepared prior to receiving any calls. You do not want even one little thing to disrupt your interview process or how you are perceived.

VOICE MAIL AND PHONE TIPS

- Make sure the outgoing voice mail message (on all contact numbers) has your voice, and your voice *only*, recorded in a clear, professional manner. No poetry. No shenanigans. No five-minute song. You want them to take you seriously. The music, the blues, the poetry, and the inspiring word of the day should all go.
- As long as your résumé is circulating, always answer the phone with energy, enthusiasm, and in

a professional, friendly manner, regardless of the time. First impressions are critical, and you never know when an employer is going to call. "Turning it on" after you have realized who is calling is often too late. Keep in mind, interviewers may call you early in the morning, in the evening, or on the weekends. Always be prepared.

- Once you've started circulating your résumé, check your messages frequently (at least three times a day) or forward your calls to yourself directly if you are out. As a last alternative, leave a forwarding number. Remember to make it as easy as possible to be contacted.

- Make sure your contact numbers are your contact numbers, not family, or friends who might not relay an important message. You will often only get one call.

- Return all calls promptly to convey your interest.

- Haven't gotten any calls since you submitted your résumé?

  - Check your e-mail (including your spam folder). Employers often reach out initially electronically.

  - Verify that the call back number on your résumé is correct.

  - Verify that your phone is not blocked for privacy. Keep unblocked for the duration of the interview process. Managers often have private numbers and will not disclose them to someone they don't know.

- Any privacy-call services requiring extra time (and patience) from the caller should be avoided. Most managers are very pressed for time and may not wait. (A few more solicitation calls won't hurt you.)

FACEBOOK AND OTHER WEB-BASED PERSONAL-INFORMATION TIPS

Make sure whatever information you have posted on the Internet and is visible to others represents you in a highly professional manner. This includes pictures, postings, comments, nicknames, political or religious viewpoints, etc. If these things do not represent you in a strictly professional, largely neutral manner, remove them. Set your privacy settings so the general public can't view your information or simply shut it down entirely for the duration of your interview process. Do all of this *prior to* commencing your job search. Interviewers surf the net too. You don't want such information (however minor you may feel it is) to disqualify you.

Section II, Chapter 3

PREPARING A BRAG BOOK

WHAT IN THE WORLD IS A BRAG BOOK?

A brag book is simply a compilation of your accomplishments. It should be in a professional and well-organized format.

PURPOSE

The purpose of your brag book is to provide tangible examples (proof) of who you are and what you've done. Companies look for a consistent history of performance and accomplishments. A brag book serves to support the claims you have made about yourself. Be prepared to show it as a proof source and review highlights. Keep in mind the "product" the company is buying is *you*, not your brag book, so don't use it as a crutch or dwell on it excessively during an interview; instead, use it as a reference to highlight key talking points during your interview. If interviewers want to spend more time reviewing the information, they will let you know. Interviewers can also review it after the interview on their own.

WHAT TO INCLUDE AND SUGGESTED ORDER OF APPEARANCE

- Cover page including your name, contact information, company, and position for which you are being interviewed, and interview date
- Résumé and contact information
- Summary of qualifications
- Ranking and any key performance data (hard data including sales numbers, attainment goals, etc.), data must be favorable
- Performance evaluations (if they are favorable)
- Recognition and award information (copies of announcements, certificates, even pictures of awards)
- Letters of commendation from
  - Immediate supervisor
  - Management or related department heads
  - Key customers
  - Academic principals
- Related accomplishments, articles, programs completed, certificates earned, etc.
- Any information that is an outstanding reflection of you.

You may organize performance and letters of commendation information with most recent accolades first (reverse-chronological order) or with most significant information first, whichever reflects your accomplishments best.

All brag book information must be accurate.

Note: Plan to leave a copy or copies of your brag book with the interviewer or interviewers. Be sure to bring appropriate number of copies to your interview and keep originals in a safe place.

BRAG BOOK FORMAT OPTIONS

- Neat, professional format (avoid loose papers)
- Report or other professional-looking presentation folder
- Binder (for a lot of information)
- Spiral bound version may be done inexpensively at a copy center
- Labeled divider tabs to segment various categories for ease of reference
- Key areas highlighted so you can reference key information quickly during your interview and maintain interviewer's focus

For tips on how to present, see "Present Your Brag Book" in "Things to Do" section, (Section III, Chapter 3).

PREPARING FOR QUESTIONS

EFFECTIVE PREPARATION

Great news! Outlined in this book are all the tools needed to help you prepare for the questions and answers on your interview. Having come this far in reading *How to Ace a Job Interview!* you already have the fundamental concepts required to respond expertly to virtually any question that may be asked.

You learned what employers are looking for and the importance of doing the necessary homework on yourself and the company prior to your interview so that you have the knowledge and information needed to respond effectively to any question. Five of the Seven Fundamentals include specific information on how to interact and respond thoroughly to interviewer questions.

Review your completed *Greatest Strengths Worksheet*, your résumé, and the homework you have done on yourself and the company. Should difficult questions still arise, always reflect on the *dating analogy* for guidance.

Also review and incorporate the following information from "The Seven Fundamentals" (Section I, Chapter 4):

- Fundamental Rule #1: Knowledge of What You Want
  - Refer to information on: knowing what and why
- Fundamental Rule #2: A Clear Understanding of the Job
  - Refer to information on: doing your homework on the company
- Fundamental Rule #3: The Necessary Background and Skill Set
  - Refer to information on: doing your homework on yourself, *Greatest Strengths Worksheet*, Past Behavior Rule, and explaining job changes
- Fundamental Rule #4: High Level of Motivation and Enthusiasm
  - Refer to information on: maintaining a high level of enthusiasm
- Fundamental Rule #5: A Positive Attitude
  - Refer to information on: responding to questions about weaknesses, past failures, and staying positive

So put away the anxiety (and the list of 1,001 study questions), especially if time is of the essence, and remember what you have already learned in this book.

You have everything you need. Just be sure to follow the steps outlined!

Section II, Chapter 5

PREPARING YOUR OWN QUESTIONS

Interviewing is a two-way street. You can, and should gather information too. Just remember, the interviewer has the right of way.

THE PURPOSE OF ASKING QUESTIONS

- Appropriate questions (both prior to and during an interview) enable you to learn more about the job itself and your fit with the company.

- The more information you gather, the better you can position yourself as the ideal fit for a particular position.

- Questions convey interest. The more you know and actively learn about a company and position, the more you are communicating interest to the interviewer.

- An absence of questions can be perceived as a lack of interest. (Imagine a first date where your date didn't ask you anything. The same holds true from an interviewer's perspective).

PREPARING QUESTIONS

While the majority of questions will be directed toward you on an interview, you should be prepared with your own questions as well. Due to time constraints, you should prioritize your questions and make sure the ones you do ask have the greatest impact (both in terms of gathering information, as well as making a positive impression on the interviewer). Familiarizing yourself with the following two categories of questions will help you develop appropriate, high-impact, quality questions for your upcoming interview.

CATEGORIES OF QUESTIONS

BASIC FACT-FINDING (PRE-INTERVIEW) QUESTIONS

These should always be answered *prior to* your interview.

- Uncover general preliminary information, such as a company's mission, values, products or services, recent news, and information, etc.
- Yield information that is easily obtained through the Internet (or other means).
- Serve as the foundation for your on-interview/ in-depth questions.
- Avoid asking these on your interview. Gather the information ahead of time.

IN-DEPTH (ON-INTERVIEW) QUESTIONS

These should be asked on your interview.

- Questions based on information you have already obtained on the industry, company, and position.
- Developed upon completion of your homework and should be asked during your interview.
- Help create a more in-depth understanding on the company, its environment, and the position, which allows you to more effectively describe how you are a perfect fit.
- Demonstrate to the interviewer you have done your homework, simply by virtue of the fact that you knew enough information to ask the more in-depth question.
- The majority of your on-interview questions should be in depth questions. Prepare and prioritize your list of questions. (If time runs short, you will be able to ask the most important ones).
- Always be respectful of the interviewer's time and keep your questions to a reasonable number.

SITUATION:

Candidate on an interview for a sales position

INAPPROPRIATE INTERVIEW QUESTIONS (BASIC FACT-FINDING/PRE-INTERVIEW QUESTIONS):

1. "What products and/or services does your company have?"
2. "How long have you been in business?"

RATIONALE:

These are inappropriate interview questions as they demonstrate an overall lack of preparedness. Such basic fact-finding questions show that the candidate made no effort at all to learn abobut the company and can even be insulting. In most instances, the candidate could have and should have looked this information up prior to the interview.

APPROPRIATE INTERVIEW QUESTION (IN-DEPTH, ON-INTERVIEW QUESTION):

"With regard to your number one product, XYZ, I understand you have two main competitors, ABC and DEF. What challenges are you facing currently with regards to these competitors and how are you responding to their entry into the market?"

RATIONALE:

The candidate demonstrates an awareness of the company's key product and competitors. This question, in and of itself, indicates that the candidate did important preliminary homework on the company prior to the interview. This conveys a heightened level of interest and preparedness to the interviewer.

SPECIFIC TYPES OF QUESTIONS TO ASK

- *Open-Ended, Opinion-Related (Non-Yes/No) Questions.* This type of question allows interviewers to talk freely and help you gather more information than yes-no questions do. They help provide a "bigger picture" since you can ask multiple people the same question and get a wide range of perspectives.

- *Career-Oriented Questions.* These show an interest in having a future with the company, which makes you appear more stable. By expressing interest in promotion, you are inferring you will work hard to get there.

- *Challenge-Related Questions.* These convey an awareness that challenges may exist, give you an opportunity to demonstrate a sense of fearlessness, and explain how you have the skills to meet those challenges.

- *Virtually Any Question You Wish.** Just be sure to ask with optimism, enthusiasm, and interest. (*See exceptions below).

*QUESTIONS TO AVOID ASKING

- *Basic Fact-Finding/Pre-Interview Questions.* Questions that uncover basic facts should be answered prior to the **interview**.

- *(Highly) Personal Questions.* These may make an interviewer uncomfortable, so don't risk it. If you are unsure as to where to draw the line, avoid personal questions entirely.
- *Salary-Related Questions.* While money is important, it shouldn't be brought up too early (unless the interviewer initiates the discussion). Salary-related questions may convey that money is your primary concern, which isn't the impression you want to give. If, for example, your date asked you how much money you made and what you had to offer your first time out, how would you feel? An interviewer will feel the same way when salary is brought up too early, no matter what the intent. So before you get into money discussions, allow the interviewer to get to know you, trust you, and see your worth (see "Getting the Offer").
- *Questions Expressing-Doubt.* You can ask virtually any question you want, so long as it is asked with interest and enthusiasm. Never express doubt or negativity (even if you have some). Expressing doubt may cause the interviewer to see you as unsure about the position, easily discouraged, and possibly even disgruntled. Asking with interest and enthusiasm, while giving you the same answer, it won't trigger any flags in the interviewer's eyes. Even if you ultimately decide the position is not for you, you want to keep that decision in your hands.

SITUATION:

During your research, you learned the company you will be interviewing with recently had a major product recall, which could affect your ability to earn commission. You are not comfortable with this news and want to determine whether this position is still a viable fit for you.

INAPPROPRIATE QUESTION:

"How in the world am I going to make any money with you since you just lost your big seller?"

RATIONALE:

The response is filled with doubt and skepticism, which trigger doubts in the interviewer about you, your commitment to, and interest in the company. So even if your concerns are subsequently addressed, you have diminished the likelihood of moving forward in the interview process because you have lost value as a candidate.

APPROPRIATE RESPONSE:

"You've got an excellent sales team, but had a difficult situation with the recent product recall. How has this affected the company and what challenges do you see in maintaining your existing high growth?"

RATIONALE:

This (more appropriate) response is much more positive and optimistic. There are no traces of doubt, and the interviewer will see you as an individual with a very positive attitude who is not easily discouraged. You will get your answer either way, but this response will keep you in a favorable standing with the interviewer.

IMPORTANT NOTE:

- Write out your list of basic fact-finding questions and make every effort to gather this information through research prior to your interview.
- Write your list of in-depth (on-interview) questions to bring to your interview.
- Organize questions in priority order; highlight those that are essential.
- Continue to add to your list as you do your research.
- Bring list of questions to your interview.

For additional information, refer to "Things to Ask and Say" in the *On-Interview* section, (Section III, Chapter 2)

ARRIVAL AND ATTIRE

This chapter includes those things you must physically do (or not do) on your interview. What you don't know can hurt you. Don't underestimate this information! Factors, such as arrival time and attire, however subtle, can have a major impact on an interviewer's perception of you and their subsequent decision to move forward with you or not. Failure to follow even one of the following suggestions can derail an interview. You want to be careful to create a positive impression and keep things on the right track.

ARRIVE EARLY (NOT ON TIME, EARLY!)

- This is absolutely essential. Even a minute late, no matter what the excuse, can often be a deal breaker.
- Allow time for extra traffic, earthquake, fire, or flood, then, multiply it by two.
- Alleviate the unnecessary stress or risk associated with being late.
- Allow for any preliminary paperwork to be completed, or even to begin the interview early.

- If you have any doubt about your ability to get to your interview on time, stay in a local hotel the evening before. (Some companies will reimburse for such expenses when traveling from out of town, but don't press the issue.)
- Allow time to visually check yourself in a full-length mirror. Hair, teeth, eyes, clothes, etc. You want to look your best and avoid any embarrassing surprises.

APPROPRIATE PROFESSIONAL ATTIRE

- Perceptions influence decisions. Like most of us, interviewers form impressions very quickly. You want the interviewer to see you for your strengths, not be distracted by anything over which you have control.
- Determine what is "appropriate."
- Observe existing company employees in similar positions.
- Stay in fashion, but don't try to make a statement.
- When in doubt, err on the conservative side.

ATTIRE FOR WOMEN*

- Blue or black business suit, (jacket, pants, skirt, blouse)
- Nylons
- Polished, low to medium heeled shoes

- Light jewelry is okay (neck and ears only, single earring per ear)
- Neutral nail polish (not too bright)
- Conservative hairstyle: "under control" and out of your face (if your hair is very long, you may want to pull it back)
- Minimal make up is okay (conservative colors)
- Little or no perfume (recommend *no*)

ATTIRE FOR MEN*

- Generally recommend a charcoal gray or navy suit (avoid sport coat and slacks and keep your jacket on. Don't get too casual)
- Solid color tie (patterned ties are okay, but not too flashy)
- Wear an undershirt (helps with perspiration)
- Minimal jewelry (a watch or wedding band is okay)
- Neat, clean-cut, conservative hairstyle
- Neatly trimmed moustache or clean-shaven
- Avoid goatees (or excessive facial hair in general)
- Polished dress shoes (black, brown, or burgundy with matching belt)
- Little or no cologne (Recommend *no*)

Note: Formality of attire can vary by profession and position, so there are exceptions to these guidelines. Keep in mind, however, it is always better to be overdressed than underdressed.

PHYSICAL TIPS FOR ALL

- Be well groomed
- Clean teeth and fresh breath (always check!)
- Neatly combed, trimmed hairstyle
- Well-maintained, manicured nails
- Pressed garments
- Turn off your cell phone
- Remove your bluetooth
- Remove your sunglasses
- No tinted glasses
- Be sufficiently hydrated
- If you tend to get nervous, apply non-glossy lip balm to prevent dry lips

For additional information on physical tips refer to "Body Language" in the *On the Interview* section. (Section III, Chapter 4)

Section II, Chapter 7

A FEW FINAL PRE-INTERVIEW POINTERS

- Verify Interview Specifics
  - Date, time, and location
  - Interviewer's name and title
  - Have interviewer contact information (if possible)
  - Company, products, and/or services
  - Determine if there are any other special requirements

- Schedule Time Off Whenever Possible
  - Full or partial day
  - Prevent potential conflicts
  - Reduce stress associated with other obligations
  - Allows you to focus on the interview at hand

SECTION III

ON THE INTERVIEW

SECTION III, CHAPTER 1

THINGS TO BRING

It is essential you demonstrate a high level of professionalism and preparedness in everything you do, including planning and organizing for your interview. The appearance of disorganization can be a deal breaker.

KEY THINGS TO BRING ON YOUR INTERVIEW

- At least three to five copies of your résumé. Interviewer's copy, your copy, and a few extras. If it is a panel-style interview, you will want to bring the appropriate number of copies based on the number of interviewers expected. You can often confirm this information when the interview is initially scheduled.
  - Your copy serves as a reference or "cheat sheet." You never want to have to ask the interviewer if you can see your own résumé to confirm details. Best to have it easily accessible or in front of you.
  - Extra copies are for additional interviewers that may sit in.
- Brag Book. See "Preparing a Brag Book" in Pre-Interview Preparation, (Section II, Chapter 3).

- Daily Planner, Electronic or Other Organizer
  - Whatever means you use to keep track of your plans and schedule, bring it.
  - These tools demonstrate your sense of organization and allow you to confirm availability and schedule future appointments on the spot. If an interviewer wants to see you again, you don't want to have to check and get back to them if you can avoid it.
- Note Pad
  - Recommend using a note pad or planner for notes. Be sure to take notes and never use scrap paper!
  - Do not recommend using Blackberry or other electronic devices for note taking.
- Prioritized List of Questions. See "Preparing Your Own Questions" in the Pre-Interview Preparation, Section II, Chapter 5.
- A Pen, plus an extra one. The last thing you need to be concerned about is a pen running out of ink. The pen should be professional in appearance. Even little things like this can make a big difference in an interviewer's perception of you.
- A Positive Attitude! Be *sure* to bring this with you!

Note: Academic, driving, and credit records are generally not required during the early phases of the interviewing process. Employers will notify you when they need them.

Section III, Chapter 2

THINGS TO ASK AND SAY

Think before you speak. A spoken word cannot be recalled. Remember the seven fundamentals.

BEGIN WITH A SINCERE ACKNOWLEDGMENT

Thank the interviewer for meeting with you.

GATHER INFORMATION

- Throughout the interview, as opportunity permits, ask open-ended, information-gathering questions (questions that require more than a yes-no response).
- Ask closed yes-no questions to confirm what you've learned.
- Ask the interviewer about the company, the position, challenges, opportunities, etc. (See "Preparing Your Own Questions" in the Pre-Interview Preparation section, (Section II, Chapter 5).
- Gain an understanding of what it takes to succeed. This will allow you to more precisely describe how your greatest strengths align perfectly with the requirements of the job.

- Inquiring about an interviewer's career path, professional choices, successes, challenges, etc., can provide some insightful information. People generally like to talk about themselves (including interviewers), but play this by ear as not all interviewers are willing to share. If you do engage, keep the primary focus of your conversation around work.

IF YOU NEED AN ICE-BREAKER

While your primary focus should be on the interview itself, an acknowledgment of any visible office paraphernalia such as awards, sports, photos, etc., at the beginning of an interview can be an effective segue into your interview, so long as your comments are sincere and brief.

SPEAK WITH CONFIDENCE AND OPTIMISM

- Be positive with your words, tone, and inflection.
- Speak clearly and audibly. Exude confidence.
- When discussing challenges you have faced, stick with facts and never express bitterness or negativity. Make sure the last words out of your mouth are always positive.
- Keep answers solution-oriented. Explain how you overcame the problem and improved the situation. Never focus on the problem.

- If you can't explain and support something, don't bring it up.

NEVER SAY ANYTHING NEGATIVE ABOUT YOURSELF

You've heard this before, but it is worth repeating.

- Present yourself as the "perfect picture" of their ideal candidate.
- *You* must be your biggest advocate!
- Maximize your positives.
- Minimize your negatives.

BE PREPARED TO DISCUSS YOUR WEAKNESSES

- You must minimize your weaknesses (to the point of zero).
- In response to a perceived drawback, explain how you actually do have that requirement (if you do) and support with tangible examples.
- If you do not possess a particular requirement, explain what you do have, minimizing the drawback by substituting an alternate, even greater example of a strength.
- Turn every "weakness" into a positive. Remember, "What's your greatest weakness?" is a trick question. It is not the time to spill out all of your flaws or even a single flaw. Rather, take this as an opportunity to demonstrate your strengths.

- Refer to "Fundamental Rule #5," (Section I, Chapter 4, "The Seven Fundamentals."

NEVER PRESENT A PROBLEM WITHOUT A SOLUTION

- You must present yourself as a problem solver.
- Every situation you have been in and every problem you describe, no matter how difficult, should be improved or solved as a result of your being involved.

EXPOSE YOUR STRENGTHS

- Be assertive with your strengths. Know them. Show them. Don't be shy and don't take them for granted. This is your time to shine. Keep in mind, sharing facts about your accomplishments is not bragging. It's critical. It is simply stating how and why you have what they require.
- Avoid hypothetical responses; use real-life examples.
- Be prepared to prove everything you say or write.
- If you don't have an example to support your claim, don't make the claim.
- Link your strengths to the company's needs.
- Always support statements and claims you make using specific, tangible examples.
- Remember the *past behavior rule*: what you share about your past is a reflection of what you will be and how you will perform in the future.

- Refer to your completed *Greatest Strengths Worksheet*, (Section V, Chapter 3)

Critical Note: You are ultimately responsible for sharing all of your key strengths. Therefore, even when the interview is coming to a close, if there is still something you wished the interviewer had asked but did not, make sure you say it. *Never leave an interview with anything critical (one of your top five or top ten greatest strengths) left unsaid.* One way to go about doing so is simply to say to the interviewer, "Excuse me, there is one more thing I would like to share with you if that's okay?" and then proceed to succinctly articulate your strength and how it will benefit the company. If the interviewer has time and is interested, he or she may take time to explore it further. If not, do not dwell on it, be careful to respect their time and close the interview.

AVOID COINED RESPONSES

Avoid coined responses like "I'm an overachiever," "I'm a perfectionist," or "I'm a people-person." They are probably in the record books for overuse. It's okay to be an overachiever, a people-person, or a perfectionist. Just use your own words to describe yourself.

ANSWER ALL OF THE INTERVIEWER'S QUESTIONS

- If you are asked a difficult question, acknowledge it as a "good" or "difficult" question and if necessary, ask for a minute to think about it. If you're truly stumped, ask if you can come back to it. Write it down, and be sure to come back with an answer.

- Never avoid a question. Interviewers note everything. Even if you forget to come back to it, they won't.
- By completing the *Greatest Strengths Worksheet*, you will be able to answer virtually any question.
- Never answer hastily. Get it right the first time. You can never retract what you've said.
- Be specific and to the point with your answers.

WHEN TO ASK QUESTIONS

- *Throughout the Interview.* Remember, questions indicate interest. Follow the interviewer's lead and be careful not to "take over."
- *At the End of the Interview.* Always plan to have at least a few more questions at this point. Interviewers expect you to have them. Questions here convey continued interest and express your understanding that there is always more to learn.
- *Questions to Avoid Asking.*
  - Basic Fact-Finding, Pre-Interview Questions.
  - Questions Expressing Doubt.

- (Highly) Personal Questions.
- Salary-Related Questions.
- Also see "Preparing Your Own Questions" in the *Pre-Interview Preparation* section, (Section II, Chapter 5 for full details)

DISCUSSING SALARY

WHEN TO DISCUSS SALARY

- If you are working with a recruiter, the recruiter will generally provide you with salary and benefits information up front.
- Initiating salary discussions with hiring managers is generally not recommended.
- Salary discussions should ideally be initiated by the employer.
- If the initial phone screener is not the hiring manager, you can confirm salary range at the conclusion of the phone screen.
- Any negotiations regarding salary should occur only after the company has come to recognize your value and has clearly stated they want you. This is normally at the point of an offer. (See "Getting the Offer," Section IV, Chapter 3)
- List your desired salary range on any application forms.
- If your salary requirements are significantly above the company's range, you may want to find a more suitable position or company.

WHAT IF SALARY AND BENEFITS INFORMATION IS NOT DISCUSSED?

It is, of course, helpful to know upfront the salary and benefits information of whatever position for which you are interviewing, but it can be a sensitive subject. If you have been unable to obtain this information from the company or another source and need to know in advance of an actual offer, an effective, sensitive approach is to first reiterate your interest in the opportunity and then politely inquire. For example, "I am very interested in this opportunity and look forward to the next steps in the process. One thing I didn't ask about was the benefits package. Can you give me a ballpark figure of what the salary/overall compensation/ benefits plan might look like?" This takes some of the edge off, so it doesn't appear as if salary is your only concern and should get you the information you are seeking.

For additional information on things to say during your interview, also reference the following sections and/ or chapters:

- The Dating Analogy, Section I, Chapter 3
- The Seven Fundamentals, Section I, Chapter 4
- Preparing for Questions, Section II, Chapter 4
- Preparing Your Own Questions, Section II, Chapter 5
- Closing the Interview, Section III, Chapter 6

THINGS TO DO

*T*hink before you act. Think positively. Your actions and results will follow your thoughts.

BELIEVE IN YOURSELF!

- Know who you are and never give up!
- Reflect on your greatest strengths for reassurance. (A thorough review of your completed *Greatest Strengths Worksheet* prior to your interview will give you the boost you need.)
- Remember you are "picture perfect" for the position!
- Stay positive.

BE HONEST

- Never misrepresent yourself.
- Never withhold requested information.* "I'm not comfortable sharing that" for example is one of the quickest ways to destroy trust and credibility. Barring an entirely inappropriate question of a highly personal nature, if they ask, answer.* Remember, you must develop a trusting relationship with the interviewer.

Don't worry, interviewers have rules they must follow and, generally, won't or can't ask just anything.

*If an interviewer is asking highly inappropriate or illegal questions, unrelated to the job such as those surrounding race, religion, gender preferences, nationality, disabilities, or other such questions, not only are you not obligated to answer, but you should seriously consider whether an environment that does not abide by laws, moral or ethical standards is one in which you wish to become a part of.

Note: Being honest does not mean opening the floodgates and sharing every imperfect thing about yourself. In fact, you should never express anything imperfect about yourself. Simply be truthful with the information that you do share, and share the positive aspects of yourself and your experiences.

KNOW YOUR RÉSUMÉ

- Be prepared to explain everything you have written!
- Support with tangible examples (proof sources).

BE SENSITIVE TO THE INTERVIEWER'S NEEDS

- Follow their lead.
- Respect their time.
- Listen actively and answer the question at hand directly and succinctly.

- Read their body language and respond appropriately. For example, if an interviewer appears ready to move on to another question, wrap up your statement succinctly and allow the interviewer to proceed with the interview.
- Shorten or extend answers depending on the interviewer's interest and response.
- Use the interviewer's name periodically.

LISTEN ACTIVELY!

BE YOURSELF, BUT NEVER FORGET YOU'RE ON AN INTERVIEW!

- While developing an open, trusting relationship is essential, never forget where you are.
- Be comfortable, but not too comfortable.
- Always maintain a friendly but professional dialog, keeping the interaction professional.
- Interviewers often deliberately create a relaxed atmosphere for a candidate to put their guard down and show their true colors.
- Discussing things in common with the interviewer can be very positive. Generally, however, follow the interviewer's lead with regards to how much personal information to disclose.
- Never say or do anything you wouldn't want to be evaluated on.

TAKE NOTES

- Notes indicate interest; be sure to take them.
- Jot down key points, questions, and follow-up items as they arise.
- Notes should be taken in brief intervals so you don't lose important eye contact.
- If you are at all uncomfortable about note taking, simply ask up front, "Do you mind if I take notes?" The interviewer will oblige you, and you can take notes with peace of mind.
- Don't take notes during an interview on any device that requires typing.

SHOW YOUR INTEREST AND ENTHUSIASM!

- A "hungry" candidate is an excellent candidate. Sincere interest and enthusiasm combined with light experience can actually outweigh low enthusiasm with a great deal of experience.
- Body language and manner of speaking should convey enthusiasm.
- Smile occasionally.

PRESENT YOUR BRAG BOOK

For information on preparing your Brag Book, see Section II Chapter 3.

- Refer to your Brag Book during or at end of interview.
- Use as a general or specific reference to support (not replace) your verbal claims.
- Do not attempt to review every detail.
- Be considerate of the interviewer's time. Don't "data dump."
- In sections with heavy text, specifically point out any information you had previously highlighted to help the interviewer focus on what you want them to see.
- Be prepared to briefly explain data or unfamiliar terms (such as company acronyms).
- If you have performed well, but a previous employer didn't furnish any or all of this supportive information, simply explain so during the interview. If you lack this information due to a poor performance issue, be prepared to explain the situation and how you have improved or grown from the experience.
- Provide a copy for your interviewer to keep. Keep all originals!

ALWAYS REFLECT ON THE DATING ANALOGY

- Whenever you are "stuck" and unsure what to do or say
- As a rule of thumb, so you will always know how to respond appropriately

PANEL INTERVIEWS

Occasionally, companies conduct a panel interview where several people interview a candidate simultaneously. The dynamic is only slightly different than a one-on-one interview.

Keep the following things in mind for an effective panel interview.

- When asked a question, share your answer with all interviewers.
  - When responding, give about 60 percent face time to the person that asked the question and 40 percent to the other(s).
  - Since each interviewer will be evaluating you, it is important they all feel included, even if one person is in a strictly observational role. The only exception to this is if an individual is in a conspicuously out of the way location in the room.
- Bring appropriate copies of your résumé, brag book, etc., for all interviewers.
- Deliberately relax. Remind yourself it's just a conversation with a group of people. You are simply sharing with them who you are, what you've done, and what you can do for their organization.
- You may ask specific questions to individual interviewers, but when you are closing, confirm you have addressed all their questions as a group

and close them all as a group. Ask for all their contact information.

- Don't forget to close! (See the "Closing the Interview," Section III, Chapter 6).

PHONE INTERVIEWS

Companies will often conduct an initial phone interview (or phone screen) ahead of an in-person interview. These should be treated with the same level of seriousness as you would an in-person interview. Follow the same overall guidelines insofar as pre-interview, on-interview, and post-interview planning as outlined in this book. Be extra careful to maintain a high level of energy and enthusiasm and to speak audibly and deliberately, since without visual cues, interviewers will place a greater emphasis on your voice. Be sure to have the following in front of you for reference during your phone interview:

- A working pen
- A note pad
- Copy of your résumé
- Completed *Greatest Strengths Worksheet*
- Your calendar (so you can schedule your face-to-face interview, which will surely follow!)

One of the great benefits to a phone interview is that you can have your *Greatest Strengths Worksheet* right in front of you and can check each strength off as you discuss it!

Plan ahead. Find a quiet place away from any potential disturbances.

Don't forget to close!

JOB FAIR INTERVIEWS
(INTERVIEWING AT THE EXHIBIT BOOTH)

Job fairs are designed to allow you to learn more about multiple job opportunities at once. They also allow employers to get a quick snapshot of dozens, if not hundreds, of potential candidates. These interviews are typically held at or near the booth and generally speaking, time is of the essence to make an impression. It is therefore critical to:

- Know your top five greatest strengths
- Have specific, succinct, tangible examples to support each
- Be prepared to quickly summarize your "why you?" statement. (What makes you the best person for the job?)
- Be able to quickly reference any key highlights on your résumé

You will generally have anywhere from two to fifteen minutes (if you're lucky) to communicate your interest and qualifications in this type of a setting. If possible, to maximize your experience, gather as much preliminary information as you can, as you would for a regular interview.

You will often have a limited amount of time to gather information at the booth or from the interviewer.

Depending on the arrangement, some career fairs schedule interviews in advance. This is optimal, as you will generally have more time to spend with an interviewer. Treat these as you would a normal interview, following all of the interview principles outlined in this book.

Don't forget to close!

VIDEO (REMOTE) INTERVIEWS

Companies occasionally conduct video conference-style (remote) interviews to accommodate geographical limitations and tight timelines. In this type of interview, the interviewer and interviewee interact via a televised screen instead of in person. Generally speaking, the same key rules apply for remote interviews as for in-person interviews. There are, however, a few unique nuances to be aware of both prior to and on the interview.

PRIOR TO INTERVIEW:

- Make sure interviewer has received copies of all pertinent information, including your résumé, Brag Book, and all key documents or information to which you plan to refer during your interview since you can't hand it to the interviewer in person.
- Secure a quiet, private, area with video-conferencing capabilities

- Be sure the desk and area behind you are clear and clean. No visible clutter should appear on screen
- Dress as you would for an in-person interview
- Eliminate or minimize any potential distractions
- Neatly organize any documents and materials you may need at your desk for easy access, including your résumé, a note pad, pen, Brag Book highlights and a list of key questions. (You don't want to be searching for information once the interview begins).
- Practice in advance with a friend who can give constructive feedback on how you appear on-camera, including eye contact, hand gestures, background, lighting, and sound quality.

DURING THE INTERVIEW

- Except for note-taking or briefly glancing at a document, maintain excellent visual contact with the interviewer. Keep in mind, if there are distractions around you and you look away from the camera, all the interviewer will see is you looking around. Stay focused for a distraction-free interview.
- Project your voice
- Of course, don't forget to close!

BODY LANGUAGE

Employers consciously and subconsciously notice your verbal and physical cues. They make decisions based on your physical responses and appearance. Make sure these cues compliment rather than diminish you. You want to create a positive, first, and lasting impression.

APPROPRIATE BODY LANGUAGE

On the day of your interview, from the moment you enter the premises to the moment you leave, you are subject to physical inspection. First impressions are lasting impressions and are not easily undone. An interviewer may see you long before you see them, so it is important your body language consistently conveys professionalism, poise, and interest. Know what your body language is saying about you at all times. Don't underestimate the impact of this!

Outlined below are the key areas to be cognizant of with regards to body language.

It begins with eye contact.

MAINTAIN EXCELLENT EYE-CONTACT

- Communicate sincerity
- Communicate interest to the interviewer regarding the company and the opportunity
- Think of the *dating analogy*
- Deliberately block out distractions and stay focused; just a glance away at the wrong time can send the wrong message

FIRM HANDSHAKE

- This can make a deliberate statement about you
- It is a critical part of the first impression (following initial visual observation)
- Apply appropriate firmness
  - Not a bone crusher (which conveys aggression and/or dominance)
  - Not a "wet fish" (which conveys insincerity and/or lack of self confidence

IMPORTANT TIP ABOUT HAND SHAKE-EYE CONTACT

When you are shaking hands, never break eye contact before releasing the interviewer's hand. If you glance away or begin your exit even a split second before releasing the interviewer's hand, it can send a message of insincerity and can leave a very unsettling feeling with the interviewer. Not something you want to do after completing a stellar interview. It is one of the "little things" that makes a big difference. To protect yourself from making this split second blunder, it may help to maintain eye contact for a second after releasing the interviewer's hand.

APPROPRIATE POSTURE

- Make a powerful statement both while standing *and* sitting.
- Always sit slightly forward in your chair.

IMPORTANT NOTE ABOUT SITTING FORWARD

When you are seated during your interview, your back should never touch the back of the chair. Sitting forward just a few inches makes a *significant* visual difference, conveying interest and enthusiasm versus sitting back, which conveys disengagement. (If in doubt, observe the difference in a mirror or with a friend; you will be surprised.) Managers have actually passed on candidates that sat back in their chair, specifically stating, "They didn't appear hungry enough." (Sadly, each time, the candidates thought they were simply showing they were comfortable.)

SPEAK CLEARLY AND AUDIBLY

- How you speak is a statement about yourself.
- Always use proper grammar. Don't get too comfortable. No slang.
- Project and enunciate your words for greater impact and to display confidence. (Hint: This will also help

to make you feel more confident about yourself as you hear your own voice. It works!)

- If you speak very fast, slow it down.
- If you're naturally soft spoken, turn it up.
- Mirror the interviewer. Modify the delivery of your speech to more closely reflect that of the interviewer. If an interviewer speaks more rapidly, speed up. If the interviewer speaks more slowly, slow down. (Note: Adjust only in moderation. Don't change who you are.)
- Maintain your enthusiasm.

DON'T FORGET TO SMILE!

Imagine a date with no smiles. Would you want to repeat it? You'll be surprised at what a difference a smile can make.

For additional information pertaining to Body Language, also reference the following sections and chapters:

- The Dating Analogy, Section I, Chapter 3
- Arrival and Attire, Section II, Chapter 6

DEALING WITH FEAR

We interact with people we know are fearful very differently than we do with those we see as threatening.

M any people think of an interview as a fearful experience and interviewers as the producers of that fear. This chapter offers a very different perspective, one designed to change the way you view and approach interviewing, interviewers, and how you respond to fear itself.

A DIFFERENT PERSPECTIVE

Despite the intimidating gaze you may receive from the other side of the desk, there are very real underlying concerns driving an interviewer's behavior. A company's success is contingent upon its ability to hire and retain good people. The consequences of a bad hire can be devastating. This responsibility falls on the interviewer and along with this responsibility comes the fear of misjudging someone and making a mistake. What if you are not who you say you are, or can't do what you say you can do?

Virtually, all of an interviewer's questions, therefore, are designed to help alleviate those underlying fears. Of course, the greater the underlying fear, the more intense the questions will be. The key is to effectively identify and address the concerns, not to be thrown off by the intensity of the questions.

HOW TO ADDRESS FEAR

The antidote to fear is reassurance, whether it is a child, a friend, or an interviewer. The more fear someone has, the more reassurance is needed, simple as that. Reassurance requires support. For an interviewer, this means providing supportive examples of the claims you are making about yourself and your abilities. (See your *Greatest Strengths Worksheet.*) These examples let the interviewer know that you are who you say you are, can do what you say you can do, and have the experience needed to be successful with their company.

By presenting yourself as the *solution* to the interviewer's concerns, the interviewer's fears will be reduced or eliminated, and the interviewer will feel comfortable in recommending that you move forward in the interview process.

THE TRICKY PART

To the outside observer, interviewers don't *appear* fearful at all. Instead, they may appear challenging, reluctant, skeptical, stubborn, or even threatening. When you are faced any of these façades, don't think for a second that you are failing or are faced with an insurmountable hurdle. Instead, see this is an opportunity to look beyond the façade, share your best supportive examples, and erase the interviewer's fears. Help the interviewer realize the best thing that could have happened to their company just sat down in front of them.

DEALING WITH YOUR OWN FEAR

The best thing you can do to minimize or eliminate fear and anxiety on and before an interview to be prepared. By doing so, you eliminate the "what ifs" which are the primary cause of interview performance anxiety. "What if I don't know an answer?" "What if I don't have what it takes?" "What if I don't get the job?"

Thoroughly doing your homework on yourself and the company, understanding what the employer wants, and reflecting on your greatest strengths will help put these "what ifs" to rest. Knowing the multitude of unique strengths you are bringing to the table and understanding the expectations of the interviewer and how to respond to those expectations will allow you to approach your interview with a tremendous level of confidence and greater sense of calm.

If, however, you still have anxieties on your interview, following are a few simple fixes.

- Think of the interview as a simple conversation where you are talking to a good friend about who you are and what you have done
- Project your voice
- Think of something amusing for a moment
- Smile
- Breathe
- Remember your *Greatest Strengths Worksheet*
- Say a quick, silent prayer

You've got what it takes. You will be fine.

CLOSING THE INTERVIEW

Closing is an essential part of the interview process. It is also an art.

WHAT IS A CLOSE?

A close, or closing an interview, is simply asking for the next step. That next step may be the next interview, spending a day with an existing employee, or asking for the job itself. Closes consist of a specific statement or statements designed to both convey interest in moving forward and get a commitment to do so. Closing is an essential part of the interview process.

Following is an example of a close, where the candidate clearly expresses interest and specifically asks for a commitment.

> "Thank you for taking the time to speak with me. I am very interested in this position. Based on our conversation, do you have any questions or concerns regarding my background or ability to do this job?" (If no concerns, proceed to the next question). "Would you be willing to recommend that I move on to the next step in the process?"

Note: Your close should not come across as demanding, but rather as a sincere and deliberate expression of interest in moving forward in the interview process. Always be sure to use your own words.

THE IMPORTANCE OF TIMING: WHEN TO CLOSE

Closing can be done anytime during your conversation, although it is usually done toward the end of an interview, after you have had an opportunity to share all the strengths you are bringing to the table, address all of the interviewer's questions and concerns, and get the majority of your questions answered.

Since closing is more of an art than a science, there is some flexibility insofar as when you should actually close. However, closing prematurely or too forcefully can be counterproductive. Asking "When can I start?" before an employer has even suggested they will be moving you to the next stage in the interview process can be perceived as presumptuous or arrogant. It can be effective with a little humor and a smile in the right situation, but it is not generally recommended. Failure to close at all can also derail the process.

You can do a trial close to get an idea of where you stand during an interview but only after you have presented your strengths and have clearly gained the interest of the interviewer. This is not essential, but can be helpful. If you do elect to do so, limit to one and not more than two trial closes during the course of your interview. You will always have the opportunity to close at the end of the interview.

PRE-CLOSING

Prior to closing, there are a few critical steps you must take to ensure an optimal outcome.

DON'T LEAVE ANYTHING IMPORTANT LEFT UNSAID

Ideally, during the course of an interview, most of your key strengths and your specific fit with the position and company will be discussed. However, depending on the skill of the interviewer as well as other factors, this may not always occur.

If there is anything significant, such as a greatest strength, you wished the interviewer had asked during the interview but didn't, *you must tell them,* even if the interviewer is preparing to wrap up the interview. *Don't leave anything important unsaid!* It's *that* critical.

Simply tell them, "Excuse me, there's one other thing I wanted to share with you about myself/my background/ my experience…"

Then share it. But be sensitive of the interviewer's time and keep it to one or two key things.

You often have one shot to make your impression; make it count. A review of your completed *Greatest Strengths Worksheet* ahead of time will help you to know exactly what your key talking points are and what, if anything, was overlooked during the interview so you can quickly share.

VERIFY YOU HAVE ADDRESSED ALL THE INTERVIEWER'S CONCERNS

Interviewers move forward with people they are most comfortable with, so it is imperative you address all questions, eliminate any trace of doubt, and increase the interviewer's comfort level with you so that you can successfully take that next step.

Attempting to close an interviewer without first verifying you have addressed all of the interviewer's concerns is like attempting to build a house before checking to see if the foundation is set. Not a good idea. This is very risky and not advised. If there is even *one* lingering question in the interviewer's mind, the foundation for the close is not there, and your probability of getting a commitment to move on to the next step is grossly reduced.

Note: It is perfectly okay for an interviewer to have one or two questions at the end of your interview. Just be sure you uncover and address them so that you can move forward.

CRITICAL PRE-CLOSE ACTION STEPS

- Ask the interviewer if there are any remaining questions or concerns regarding your qualifications, your interest in the job, or your ability to do it.
- Address each outstanding concern enthusiastically.

- Provide supportive examples.
- Continue to ask "Is there anything else?" until the interviewer has no more questions.
- Now you're ready to close!

DON'T FORGET THE CLOSE!

Imagine your first date. Everything clicked. You spent the entire day together getting acquainted and having fun. You laughed, you shared, and you discovered how much you had in common. You bonded. You hadn't felt that positive about a match in a long time. Now, the perfect day is coming to an end and your date says "bye" and walks away. No number. No "Thanks, I had a great time." No "Can I call you?" Nothing. How would you feel? Basically, your heart would drop. You would be confused and disappointed. You might say to yourself, "I thought we had a great time together? I thought this was going somewhere…and this person just left?" You would have expected and hoped your date would have acknowledged the day, its significance, and asked when you could see each other again or at least expressed an interest in doing so. Without this, there is no closure, and you are left with a great deal of doubt and uncertainty about the individual and what just happened. This is exactly how an interviewer feels if you leave without closing them, and as you know, you never want to allow any doubt into the picture.

Overall, he was a terrific candidate. He gave solid examples of performance, described perfectly how he was qualified to excel in the position and grow with the company, but he never closed me. I won't be moving forward.

—actual hiring manager

Don't ever...repeat, *ever*, leave an interview without asking for or clearly expressing your interest in taking the next step. You decide whether a strong close or a softer close is best, but be sure to close. Express your appreciation for their time and consideration and enthusiastically reiterate your interest.

A SALES PERSPECTIVE

Some managers, particularly sales managers, no matter how well an interview goes, won't invite you back if you don't close them and ask for their card. This may sound extreme, but the reality is this: if you don't close them, why would they believe you really want the position? Why would they believe you would close your customers or get buy-in for key initiatives? Without a card or contact, how are you going to follow up? Regardless of your profession, think of your interview as a sales call where the product you are selling is you and the interviewer as your customer. As all salespeople will attest, to effectively sell a product or service, they must ask for the business. If you want the interviewer to "buy" what you are selling, you have got to close them.

KEY STEPS TO CLOSING

- Enthusiastically thank the interviewer for their time.
- Reiterate your interest in the position.
- Ask for the next step.
- Try and secure a commitment, but be sensitive to the situation and don't press too hard.
- Ask for a business card. This is very important! If they don't provide one, ask for another means of contacting them, including phone and/or e-mail so you can follow up.

Important note: Some interviewers do not provide contact information. Others won't make on-the-spot decisions with regards to next steps. This is okay. In these cases, don't press the issue. Simply asking demonstrates clear and important interest.

DON'T GIVE UP TOO SOON!

When you are preparing to close, if the interviewer expresses any hesitation or concerns about your background, experience, or ability to do the job, then ask if he or she would be willing to share those concerns, including where they feel you may have fallen short. Anytime an interviewer expresses an unwillingness to recommend you on to the next step in the interview process, provided the interviewer's concerns are not insurmountable, but rather concern matters for which you have a solution, take the following steps:

1. Emphasize your appreciation for the concern(s).
2. Present specific tangible examples of key strengths that specifically address the concern.
3. If the interviewer responds favorably confirm whether the additional information you provided addresses the outstanding concerns.
4. If the interviewer agrees, ask again if he or she would now feel comfortable recommending you on for the next step.

Throughout this exchange, pay close attention to the interviewer's expressions, body language, and overall feedback. Respond appropriately. While "pushing the envelope" is sometimes necessary, you do not want to come across as pushy or desperate. If the interviewer is unwilling to elaborate, simply thank them for their time, reiterate your interest and let the interviewer know you hope to hear from them soon. Of course ask for a business card and take all the normal post-interview follow up steps outlined in this book.

SECTION IV

POST-INTERVIEW

THANK-YOU LETTERS

A lmost there!

ARE THANK-YOU LETTERS REALLY NECESSARY?

Thank-you letters are an essential part of the interview process. Like your résumé, they are a reflection of you, must represent you professionally, and can make an excellent impression when done properly. The interview circle is not completed until your thank-you letter is sent.

Thank-you letters serve as an important reminder to the interviewer that you are still interested (like a call after a date). Don't delay. Interviewers definitely notice a candidate's follow-up and often make next step decisions the same day. You want to be sure they have your information prior to doing so. When there are two or more candidates running a close race, a prompt, professional thank-you can make the difference between who gets called back for the next interview and who does not.

WHEN SHOULD THANK YOU LETTERS BE SENT?

The sooner the better. Within twenty-four hours. Strongly recommend the same day and within the hour if possible.

FORMAT

- Typed, standard professional business format.
- Avoid hand-written cards and notes. While this is not a hard and fast rule, these are not generally recommended during the interview process, as some managers may perceive them as less professional. Whereas, all managers will openly receive a more formal, typed letter. Play it safe. Save the hand written notes for after you have received the offer if you wish. (They can be a nice touch and well received after that time.)
- Always use spell-check, double check, then recheck!

CONTENT

- Essentially, a reiteration of your interview closing remarks.
- Thank them.
- Reiterate your interest.
- Briefly mention anything particularly noteworthy that was discussed during the interview (optional).
- Briefly address anything you were to follow up on (emphasis on *briefly*).

- Let them know you hope to hear from them soon.
- Provide your e-mail and phone number (with area code) so they may contact you.

RECOMMENDED DELIVERY METHODS

- *E-mail.* Send as a Word or PDF attachment (business format) so file transfers in the same format in which you created it.
  Benefit: Immediate delivery.
- *Hand-Deliver.* Effective when interviewer is remaining at the interview location. Leave premises, prepare letter at nearby business center, and deliver to front desk or concierge.
  - Request immediate delivery to interviewer.
  - Obtain deliverer's contact information.
  - Leave premises and follow up with deliverer in five minutes to verify the letter was delivered.
  Benefit: Guaranteed immediate delivery.
- *Priority mail*: Expresses urgency. Convenient for manager. Overnight mail may be overkill.
  Benefit: Effective only if the interviewer is not making a decision the same day as the interview.
- *US-mail.* Last option due to delayed delivery.
  Benefit: Effective only if the interviewer is not making a decision the same day as the interview.
- Hand-delivery and e-mail are the best methods of delivery.

Section IV, Chapter 2

COMMUNICATION PROTOCOL

It is important you don't lose your momentum, focus, or enthusiasm during this stage.

Interviewers are still deciding.

Continued and appropriate follow-up is often what differentiates one candidate from another during this post-interview period. Do not lie dormant waiting for the phone to ring. The following communication protocol should help you keep things in perspective and keep you focused on those actions that will help set you even further apart from your competition.

Note: Always assume there is competition.

COMMUNICATION PROTOCOL

- Check voicemail and e-mail messages frequently (recommend a minimum of three to four times a day while interviewing).
- Continually demonstrate a sense of urgency. (Not panic, *urgency*.)
- Return all calls immediately! A delay at this point could cost you a subsequent interview or an offer.

- Continue to follow up with the interviewer every week to a week and a half, unless otherwise directed.
    - Brief note or call reiterating continued interest and hopes of talking with or hearing from them soon. Always leave your phone number.
- Continue with regular interval follow up until you have definitive confirmation (written or verbal) of an offer or that they will not be proceeding further with you.
- Understand the process can take some time, so don't give up too soon!
- *Stay positive*! Great things are on the way.

GETTING THE OFFER

Your phone rings. It's the call you've been waiting for. *"Congratulations! We would like to offer you the position."* This is a good day indeed! It is on its way and even may arrive sooner than you think.

BE PREPARED

Ideally, well in advance of receiving your offer, you should have an understanding of the overall benefits package and salary range for your position. While this is not always possible, it should be a goal. Salary and benefits information can be obtained from your recruiter (if you are working with one) and sometimes from the employer directly. Human Resources, interviewers, or the hiring manager are sources for this information, but as discussed previously, if the employer does not proactively share, use discretion when inquiring. Information may also be available on job posting sites, company website, or via other company employees. You should have prepared a list of pros and cons and predetermine what your minimum requirements are from a compensation standpoint. Don't wait until the last minute to start thinking about it. You may not have time. Plus, things can suddenly become very fuzzy when it comes to accepting an offer. Questions like, "Should I take it? Should I not?" "Should I ask for more money?" "Should I think about it?" may litter your mind and make an otherwise clear and simple decision very cloudy. You don't want your mind to play terrible tricks on you. You've come too far. Instead, know what you plan to do ahead of time so you have no regrets.

NEGOTIATING SALARY

Never give the impression that salary is your primary concern—even if it is. While money is important, it shouldn't be presented as more important than the intrinsic value of the job. *Note*: This is a good rule of thumb anyway.

From an employer's standpoint, it is optimal for a candidate to accept whatever offer is presented. It demonstrates a true desire to work for that company. If the employer has chosen you, they want you to want them too for who they are. Accepting a position as offered clearly conveys this. Requesting a larger package, while acceptable in many situations, can also convey to an employer that the company isn't quite good enough just as it is. To be considered acceptable, the company must up the ante. While this can be done successfully, and often is, keep in mind that you are stepping outside of the safety zone. How far out depends on you, how you present your desires, and the company's flexibility.

If you are able to determine salary and benefits information prior to receiving an offer, decide whether you want to pursue the opportunity up front based on the stated package. Some companies negotiate; others do not. If there is no room for negotiation and you already have the salary and benefits information, when the offer comes in, you can accept (or reject) it as is.

If an offer is acceptable based on your preliminary requirements, accept it.

IF OFFER IS LOWER THAN DESIRED

- As always, maintain a positive attitude.
- Enthusiastically thank them for the offer.
- Reiterate your excitement and interest in the company and the position.
- *Then* explain your desire to come in at a salary closer to $XYZ (or provide an ideal range). If you, or the hiring manager, feel it necessary to further explain this request, you can reference your own personal reasons, such as quality of life, plans to purchase a home, family needs, and so on. Avoid being too specific, but be sure to be sincere with your request.
- Await response.

By handling things in this fashion, you reassure the employer of your continued interest in the position. Employers are more willing to "go to bat" for someone with a favorable, enthusiastic attitude; but also, if the employer is unable to oblige your request, they will still feel comfortable with their decision to hire you, and you still have the option to accept the original offer if you choose.

- *Suggestion*: If an offer is below but very close to your expectations (i.e., two thousand dollars a year), you may want to simply accept it. (The after tax difference will be minimal, and you are likely to make it up in raises fairly quickly.)
- Some companies may have additional incentives available, such as signing bonuses, stock options, added vacation time, etc. If you elect to leverage these, use caution. (Such incentives are not generally available for entry-level positions.)
- *Note*: You should be aware that rejection of an offer and/or negotiation prior to receiving a your offer in writing can result in the withdrawal of that offer or, if handled improperly, can create tension between you and your new employer. Keep things in perspective. A few thousand dollars a year is not worth jeopardizing a job or a harmonious relationship with your new employer.

IF THE OFFER IS NOT ACCEPTABLE

- Use the same approach as above.
- Be prepared to walk away if your needs can't be met.
- Avoid accepting a position far below your minimum requirements if possible. It is a recipe for failure.

A FEW WORDS OF ADVICE

- Don't get greedy. It is optimal to accept an offer as is, whenever possible. (It reassures the employer they made the right choice.)
- If an offer is within your (predetermined) range, generally, you should accept it. Keep in mind that you can lose an offer as quickly as you got it.
- Purposefully remember your initial enthusiasm and what it was about the job and company that brought you to the table in the first place. Dwell on the fact you are now at the doorway of that opportunity.
- Take a moment to congratulate yourself for coming this far!

SECTION V

GET FIRED UP!

Get Fired Up!
Summary Checklist
Greatest Strengths Worksheet
Notes
About the Author

GET FIRED UP!

ON YOUR MARK...

*R*eady …You're on your way!

Okay, it's time to toss the anxiety. You are fully prepared. You've got all the tips you need!

Set…You've got what it takes!

You now have a thorough understanding of what employers are looking for from the most important perspective—an interviewer's. You have the essential insight into the rationale behind the interview process and know how to handle the little things that can make the difference between a first step and a final step. You know how to present yourself as a perfect fit and to move confidently forward in the interview. In short, you know *how to ace a job interview!* Whether you have several weeks to prepare or an interview tomorrow, reflect on these tips, and you're on your way to securing your dream job.

IF YOU NEED A BOOST

Don't forget, if you've gotten a call for an interview, you're already half way there! Don't take that lightly. Believe in yourself! Think of the interview as an opportunity to show the interviewer what you're made of, not as an insurmountable object. Simply reassure the interviewer with specific, tangible examples of why you are the best person for the job and why your experience is exactly what that interviewer needs.

Review your *Greatest Strengths Worksheet* at the end of this book as often as necessary. Take time to reflect on and appreciate the many strengths God gave you, and let them shine for the world to see or, at least, the interviewer! Know that you've got what it takes—the background, the experience, the talent, the commitment, the drive, and of course the tools to ace your interview. Never forget how valuable your unique experiences are and that the right company actually needs you too! Know it. Believe it, and the interviewer will see it also!

Never give up. Never give in! Keep a positive attitude and remain confident. Envision yourself as the picture-perfect candidate, without blemish or flaw. Once you've done your homework on yourself, the industry, and the company, you will be able to do so with unwavering confidence, no matter what challenges you are faced with. You have every reason to be confident.

Remember you're gonna get this job! Now *go out* and *ace* that interview!

SUMMARY CHECKLIST

BE SURE YOU ARE PREPARED

Verify you can affirmatively answer the following prior to your interview.

- ☐ What are your objectives?
- ☐ Have you done your homework? Do you have a clear understanding of the job, the company, its products and services, and the industry?
- ☐ Have you completed the *Greatest Strengths Worksheet*?
- ☐ Do you have recent tangible examples to support all of the following?
  - ☐ Background and skill set to do the job
  - ☐ Ability to learn the necessary information
  - ☐ Compatibility with the company and position
  - ☐ A positive attitude
  - ☐ A professional image
  - ☐ Motivation and enthusiasm
  - ☐ Specific interest in the job
  - ☐ Competence
  - ☐ Confidence
  - ☐ Determination and commitment
  - ☐ Tenacity
  - ☐ Resilience

- ☐ Assertiveness
- ☐ Ability to set and accomplish goals
- ☐ Initiative
- ☐ Excellent communication skills (including listening)
- ☐ Relationship-building skills
- ☐ Appropriate level of sensitivity
- ☐ High level of responsibility
- ☐ Ability to follow direction well
- ☐ Organizational skills
- ☐ Outstanding work ethic
- ☐ Problem solving abilities
- ☐ Ability to make an impact
- ☐ Ability to establish trust
- ☐ Professionalism
- ☐ Ability to close
- ☐ Compatibility with the interviewer
- ☐ Any other job-related skill set pertinent to the position

☐ Do you have appropriate copies of your résumé and brag book?

☐ Have you confirmed the date, time, and location of your interview?

☐ Do you know the name(s) and title(s) of interviewers? Do you have their contact information?

☐ Have you scheduled time off for your interview?

☐ Have you prepared questions for your interview?

- ☐ Have you confirmed the salary range and compensation package meet your needs and expectations?
- ☐ Have you reviewed this book in its entirety?

Then you're ready to go!

GREATEST STRENGTHS WORKSHEET

INSTRUCTIONS FOR COMPLETING

If you only have time to do one thing, do this! The *Greatest Strengths Worksheet* is one of the (if not *the*) most important exercises you can complete when preparing for an interview. A fully completed worksheet will provide you with nearly 70 percent of what an employer is looking for in an interview! It is designed to help illustrate strengths, experience, and skill-set required for the job, as well as your understanding of the job.

The ability to respond quickly and thoroughly to important interview questions with specific examples is essential! This worksheet will help to put all of your strengths and experiences at the tip of your tongue where you need them. You won't have to search for an answer. The more time you spend time with it, the more you will begin to realize just how much you have to offer. It's a very encouraging exercise in that most people discover much more about themselves and their abilities than they originally thought! Gaining this understanding helps increase one's courage muscle going into an interview.

The worksheet is designed to refresh you with *you*, decrease your anxiety, increase your confidence level, and help you effectively and precisely communicate why you are the best person for the position for which you are interviewing. It helps alleviate anxiety caused by "What ifs." ("What if I don't know an answer?") It does so because it provides you with a majority of the information you will need for answers in advance. Eliminate the "What ifs" and you eliminate the anxiety.

Upon completion of this worksheet, you will be able to describe, comfortably and thoroughly, what strengths and qualities you bring to the table and why you are the best person for the job—and prove it. Don't sell yourself short. Take as much time as you can for this exercise. The more you work on it, the more thoroughly you will cover all of your bases.

The *Greatest Strengths Worksheet* is broken down into three simple columns. (Easy as ABC!)

A: First Column: List Your Greatest Strengths

This is who you are. What you bring to the table. The essence of what an employer is looking for. List everything positive you can think about yourself here. (See "The Seven Fundamentals: What Employers Are Looking For," Section I, Chapter 4) and "*Summary Checklist*," Section V, Chapter 2). Commit to memory your top five and top ten greatest strengths. These are the most important and should always be shared on an interview. There is, however, no limit. Write as many as you can. This is an ongoing exercise. (It is also very effective if you have only minutes to prepare.) Often, other people will see strengths in you that you may take for granted. Therefore, ask friends, family, and coworkers for their input.

B: Second Column: Describe How (Strength is) Demonstrated

This is your proof source. List tangible examples that support your strength claim. Remember, anyone can claim something; not everyone can back it up with a specific, credible example. You should list at least two to three specific examples for each strength, but the sky is the limit. This way, if an inquisitive manager is pressing you, you will have several examples to share.

Proof sources (how a strength is demonstrated) must be inextricably linked to a given strength. The first time you mention a particular strength provide the supportive proof source. This adds credibility to your claim. For example, "I have consistently been recognized for my leadership abilities. Recently, I was selected by the CEO to lead all company-wide regional meetings." In this example, the strength is *leadership*, and the proof source is that you were "selected by the CEO to lead all company-wide regional meetings." If the candidate were to mention only the strength alone, it is not as impressive.

Also, a single proof source may support multiple strengths.

C: Third Column: Explain How You Will Apply Strength at the New Job

This is where you tie in who you are with what the position and company requires. Your itemized strengths must match their requirements, of course. The more closely they match, the better your chances. The less closely, the worse. It is your job to tie it all together for the interviewer. By tying things together here (The ABCs: Strengths, Proof, and How You Will Apply), you demonstrate to the interviewer your understanding of the job requirements and how you fit in perfectly.

Interviewers want to know why they should hire you. Do you have the strengths the job requires, and do you have more (quantity and quality) of them than the next candidate? It's that simple. What unique skill sets or experiences do you have that someone else does not? You will have the examples interviewers are looking for.

For maximum effectiveness, do your homework on the position, company, and industry before completing this worksheet. (Refer to Section I, Chapter 4, Fundamental Rule #2 for details on doing your homework). This will allow you to complete the third column, "How to Apply at New Job," fully and complete the exercise.

Get ready to see how good you really are! Now go out there and *ace* your interview!

HOW TO ACE A JOB INTERVIEW! by Stuart C. Taylor
GREATEST STRENGTHS WORKSHEET (It's as easy as **A, B, C!**)

A) List **YOUR GREATESTS STRENGTHS** *Minimally, know your Top 5 & 10! (Refer to "The Seven Fundamentals" & "Checklist").*	**B)** Describe **HOW THEY ARE DEMONSTRATED** *List at least 2-3 specific, supportive examples (proof sources) for each strength.*	**C)** Explain **HOW YOU WILL APPLY STRENGTHS AT NEW JOB** *Complete this after researching new job and company details/requirements.*
1.	1. 2. 3.	
2.	1. 2. 3.	
3.	1. 2. 3.	
4.	1. 2. 3.	
5.	1. 2. 3.	

HOW TO ACE A JOB INTERVIEW! by Stuart C. Taylor
GREATEST STRENGTHS WORKSHEET (It's as easy as A, B, C!)

A) List **YOUR GREATESTS STRENGTHS** Minimally, know your Top 5 & 10! (Refer to "The Seven Fundamentals" & "Checklist").	**B**) Describe **HOW THEY ARE DEMONSTRATED** List at least 2-3 specific, supportive examples (proof sources) for each strength.	**C**)Explain **HOW YOU WILL APPLY STRENGTHS AT NEW JOB** Complete this after researching new job and company details/requirements.
6.	1. 2. 3.	
7.	1. 2. 3.	
8.	1. 2. 3.	
9.	1. 2. 3.	
10.	1. 2. 3.	

NOTES

NOTES

NOTES

NOTES

NOTES

NOTES

ABOUT THE AUTHOR

Stuart C. Taylor, president of Top Performers, has a proven track record of success in the recruitment industry. He earned "Preferred Recruiter" status with multiple nation-wide firms due to the exceptional caliber of candidates he referred, all of whom he coached in preparation for their interviews. Taylor's company worked with a range of industries and also became one of the top recognized recruitment firms for the placement of pharmaceutical and medical sales professionals in the Southern California market and beyond. Taylor also has extensive experience in sales management and became a nationally ranked district sales manager with a division of Abbott Laboratories. Taylor conducts sales and interview training workshops and offers consulting services to corporations and individuals.

Please write to share your interview success stories!

For additional information, contact us at:
info@topperformers.com *or* www.topperformers.com.